LIFE WORLD LIBRARY

IRELAND

TIME LIFE BOOKS ®

LIFE WORLD LIBRARY

LIFE NATURE LIBRARY

TIME READING PROGRAM

THE LIFE HISTORY OF THE UNITED STATES

LIFE SCIENCE LIBRARY

GREAT AGES OF MAN

TIME-LIFE LIBRARY OF ART

TIME-LIFE LIBRARY OF AMERICA

FOODS OF THE WORLD

THIS FABULOUS CENTURY

LIFE LIBRARY OF PHOTOGRAPHY

LIFE WORLD LIBRARY

IRELAND

by Joe McCarthy

and the Editors of

TIME-LIFE BOOKS

TIME-LIFE BOOKS   NEW YORK

COVER: A man from the Aran
Island of Inishmore rests
beside a stone wall that runs
along the cliffs
overlooking the sea.

ABOUT THE WRITER

Joe McCarthy, author of the interpretive text for this volume of the LIFE
World Library, is an American writer and editor of Irish extraction. His father was a native of County Kerry, his mother of County Kilkenny. Mr.
McCarthy was born in Cambridge, Massachusetts. He was educated at Boston College, and worked before World War II as a reporter and sportswriter
on the now-defunct Boston *Post*. During the war he served first with the
U.S. Army artillery and then became sports editor, battle correspondent and
managing editor of *Yank*, the Army weekly, attaining the rank of master
sergeant. Since the war, Mr. McCarthy has been a frequent contributor to
American publications. His best-known book is *The Remarkable Kennedys*,
a perceptive account of the Kennedy family published in 1960. Mr. McCarthy is also the author of a number of articles on Ireland for American maga-
zines. He traveled extensively through the island in 1962 and again in 1963.

941.5
mc

© 1964 Time Inc. All rights reserved. Revised 1970.
Published simultaneously in Canada.
Library of Congress catalogue card number 64-15242.
School and library distribution by Silver Burdett Company, Morristown, New Jersey.

Contents

TIME-LIFE BOOKS

EDITOR
Maitland A. Edey
EXECUTIVE EDITOR
Jerry Korn

TEXT DIRECTOR   ART DIRECTOR
Martin Mann   Sheldon Cotler

CHIEF OF RESEARCH
Beatrice T. Dobie
PICTURE EDITOR
Robert G. Mason

Assistant Text Directors:
Ogden Tanner, Diana Hirsh
Assistant Art Director: Arnold C. Holeywell
Assistant Chief of Research: Martha T. Goolrick
Assistant Picture Editor: Melvin L. Scott

PUBLISHER
Walter C. Rohrer
General Manager: John D. McSweeney
Business Manager: John Steven Maxwell
Production Manager: Louis Bronzo

Sales Director: Joan D. Manley
Promotion Director: Beatrice K. Tolleris
Managing Director, International: John A. Millington

LIFE WORLD LIBRARY

SERIES EDITOR: Oliver E. Allen
Editorial Staff for *Ireland:*
Assistant Editor: Jay Brennan
Designer: Ben Schultz
Chief Researcher: Grace Brynolson
Researchers: Jill Adams, Sondra Albert, Barbara Ballantine, Sue Bond, Edward Brash, June Omura Goldberg, Ava Weekes, Martha Brean

EDITORIAL PRODUCTION
Color Director: Robert L. Young
Asistant: James J. Cox
Copy Staff: Rosalind Stubenberg, Helen Isaacs, Florence Keith
Picture Bureau: Dolores A. Littles, Joan T. Lynch
Art Assistants: James D. Smith, James K. Davis
Traffic: Arthur A. Goldberger

The interpretive text of this book was written by Joe McCarthy, and the picture essays were written by David S. Thomson and Edmund V. White. Many of the photographs were taken by Brian Seed. Valuable assistance was provided by the following individuals and departments of Time Inc.: LIFE staff photographer Carl Mydans; Editorial Production, Robert W. Boyd Jr., Margaret T. Fischer; Editorial Reference, Peter Draz; Picture Collection, Doris O'Neil; Photographic Laboratory, George Karas; TIME-LIFE News Service, Murray J. Gart; Reprints Editor, Paula Arno.

Introduction

It is appropriate that the LIFE World Library series on the nations of the world should devote a full volume to the Irish. Americans' affinities with both the North and South of Ireland are numerous. Many of us are Irish. Many more of us have a sympathy with Ireland defined by history and religion and the mutual experience of life on the perimeters of the North Atlantic.

As Mr. McCarthy's narrative indicates, Irishmen are proving to be among the sanest of self-governors. They have also achieved the extra energy and balance and wisdom to be a force for reason out of all proportion to their numbers. In the General Assembly, in U.N. peace-keeping operations in the Congo, in their counsel to less developed countries, their presence as a nation is freedom's good fortune. Just as the Irish and their descendants scattered through the world have in the main been the most responsible of individuals, so the Irish nation now can and does act as a responsible element in a world in which that element is all too scarce.

Trinity College and the National University of Ireland colleges in Dublin, Cork and Galway have educated many hundreds of students from the world's underdeveloped nations. Indeed, several Government leaders of the newly independent African nations have led a university life in Dublin. Although Ireland left the British Commonwealth in 1949, its Government in pre-

ceding years of association did much to define the greater flexibility of Commonwealth membership which today still binds Britain to many of its former colonies. Without Irish statesmanship such ties might not exist. Ireland, outside the Commonwealth, provided a liberal, English type of education for many Africans and Asians who, by the irony of history and nationalism, refrained from pursuing British training on British soil but eagerly absorbed it on an Irish one. With its many foreign graduates, Trinity College, established almost 400 years ago by the first Queen Elizabeth to make Irishmen good subjects of England, may have been a last, deciding factor in preserving British traditions abroad.

How these things have come about are well and stimulatingly told in Mr. McCarthy's account of Irish character and history and civilization. The beauty and charm of Ireland and its people are always evident in pictures of them, as they are in this book. If the struggle to national fulfillment has often seemed tortuous, harrowing and dark, like Ireland's weather, the irrepressible Irish personality everywhere shines through. We are fortunate to have so much of it in the United States. To learn more of Ireland, and of its modern development as well as its heritage and history, should always be an attractive enterprise for Americans. To that end it is a pleasure to introduce this book.

WILLIAM H. TAFT III
former U.S. Ambassador to the
Republic of Ireland

To the strains of a local fiddler, a girl in the regional costume joins her partner in a traditional dance for a crowd in front of the Sligo

town hall during the annual Fleadh Cheoil, or music festival.

1

In Island Isolation

AN American who looks at Ireland on a map of Europe may be surprised to find that it is such a small and isolated country. It seems unlikely that a people like the Irish, known everywhere for their songs and wit, their natural literary, political and military skills, and their unmistakable personality that sets them apart from all other nationalities, should have come from a remote little island cut off in the mists of the North Atlantic from the centers of Old World civilization.

Ireland's isolation at the cloudy crossroads where the warm air of the Gulf Stream clashes against the winds of the Arctic largely explains, however, why the Irish are different from other people. Theirs was one of the few nations in Western Europe never invaded by the Romans. The waters around them also kept out, in later centuries, other Continental refinements and helped their 700-year fight against assimilation by the English, which might have failed had Ireland been a part of the British mainland, like Wales and Scotland. Today those two nearby countries of the United Kingdom, both of which share the Celtic background of the Irish, feel little identification with Ireland.

"Some of them we may resemble in ways," an Irishman said recently of the Welsh and Scots with a certain aloof pride, "but with none of them could we be easily confused."

But island isolation cannot fully account for whatever it is that makes the Irish so distinct from everybody else; the people of Iceland, for example, are not marked with the contradictions of character that inspired G. K. Chesterton to describe the Irish as romantics whose wars are merry and whose songs are sad—and then to point out elsewhere that they excel as lawyers and soldiers because of their hardheaded realism. Another effect of a country's geography that deeply influences its temperament and spirit is the climate. If the Irish are drawn in tense suspension between bright dreams and dark reality, so is the Irish weather, which is like the weather of no other place on earth.

The weather in Ireland is too often summed up and dismissed as simply wet and cold. The writer George Moore liked to quote a Mayo farmer's complaint that his cottage was damp enough to give rheumatism to a wild duck. But the Irish seldom carry umbrellas as the British do, and the doors and windows of their country houses are always opened wide. Although it rains in Ireland almost every day, the rain seems to spend more time threatening to fall than actually falling, and when it does come, the downpour seldom lasts for more than half

---

THE COMPLEX GAELIC LANGUAGE

The language known as Gaelic, which the people of Ireland themselves refer to as "Irish," is an ancient tongue, one of the Indo-European group to which English also belongs. It is not, however, an easy language for English-speaking persons to master. Its grammar is complex. Gaelic nouns, for example, are like Latin ones in that they change their endings according to their use in the sentence. Because the language has dropped many syllables since it was given a written alphabet in the Eighth Century, and because multiple-letter combinations can make a single sound, many modern words contain letters which are not pronounced. This volume makes no attempt to utilize accent marks used in the Gaelic alphabet. Below are some common Gaelic words, and some words used in this book, with their phonetic equivalents:

Eire (Ireland): "Airuh"
Erinn go bragh (Ireland forever): "Airin go braw"
Dail Eireann (Parliament of Ireland): "Dawyl Airun"
Sinn Fein (Ourselves Alone): "Shin Fane"
Aghaidh (face): "Eye"
Fleadh cheiol (music festival): "Flah kyoil"

---

an hour. Then long, glittering beams of sunlight slant through the masses of broken gray and black clouds, and the sky may clear to a bright blue—if it does not immediately close in again, dark and mean and menacing.

Because the sky is always changing, sullen one minute and sparkling with a joyous, dancing brightness a few minutes later, the colors of Ireland's rolling countryside, usually a patchwork of many delicate shades of light and dark green, turn magically into blue, purple or gold or slide into a solemn, almost black, gray. The air, light and stimulating in the morning, may become heavy and depressing in the afternoon and clear again in the evening. In the summer months, when Ireland—on the same latitude as Labrador—enjoys late daylight, the setting sun invariably leaves the evening sky streaked with red, pink and yellow, no matter how gloomy the day may have been.

These constant changes in light and atmosphere can lift the Irishman's spirit to a carefree merriment, and then irritate him into touchy impatience with everything and everybody around him, or plunge him into dreamy, lethargic despair. "Your wits cant thicken in that soft moist air . . ." George Bernard Shaw wrote, trying to describe to an Englishman the effects of the Irish climate. "Youve no such colors in the sky, no such lure in the distances, no such sadness in the evenings. Oh, the dreaming! the dreaming! the torturing, heartscalding, never satisfying dreaming! . . ."

Because the weather weighs so heavily on the consciousness of the Irish, they talk of it endlessly with a quiet defensiveness, as if they were afraid that complaining might make it worse. On a wet day they praise the "softness" of the rain and explain to visitors that the moist coolness makes the admired complexion of young Irish women smooth and fresh. On a partly clear morning, strangers on the street cry happily to each other, "Isn't it a grand day, thanks be to God!" A slight national disapproval of rain shows itself only during the summer haying season, when sunlight becomes important to farmers. In the hurling-mad farming county of Tipperary, families end their summer prayers asking God to "beat Cork and save the hay."

The warmth of the Gulf Stream, which keeps Ireland wet, also protects it against extreme cold as its northern latitude discourages extreme summer heat. Except for a few unusual winter freezes in recent years, which some older Irish people attribute not to nuclear tests but to a deflection of the Gulf Stream by the Panama Canal, Ireland's temperatures generally stay between 40° and 60° all the year round. On some parts of the southwest coast, in Kerry and on the incredibly exotic Garnish Island in Bantry Bay, there are flourishing growths of tropical plants and palm trees. But on the same shoreline, not many miles to the north of this Gaelic Riviera, on a July day at Lahinch in Clare, an American tourist will stare at the Irish girls sprawled on the beach in brief bikinis and shudder. The air to him feels as cold as Maine in early October.

THE changing colors in the Irish sky light up and darken a variety of sharply contrasting scenic splendors below. Ireland is only about 170 miles wide and 300 miles long, a day's drive from Cork to Malin Head at the northern tip of Donegal, but it crowds into that small package almost every kind of landscape and terrain except a desert.

Almost all of the island's shoreline is fringed with steep mountain ranges. In the middle of this saucer, flowing from north to south and dividing it almost evenly in half before turning to the Atlantic at Limerick, is Ireland's Mississippi, the River Shannon. East of the Shannon,

spreading from Dublin and the wildly beautiful Wicklow Mountains up into Meath and Westmeath and down into Tipperary and Kilkenny, are rich green, rolling meadowlands which produce Ireland's superb thoroughbred horses and the hefty cattle that supply Britain with much of its beef. The fertility of this midland region is typified by the Curragh, the center of Irish horse racing in Kildare, an astonishing great plain of luxurious thick grass extending over 5,000 acres without a fence or a tree.

THE greenness of the midlands ends as they approach the Shannon and many parts of the countryside along the river's bed turn into flat and lonely brown bogs, with carefully stacked mounds of peat here and there drying for a farm cottage's fireplace. The distant horizons of the bogs are now marked with the cone-shaped smokestacks of the Irish Republic's new peat-burning electricity-generating plants.

Western Ireland, on the other side of the Shannon, is a different country altogether, no more like the plentiful midlands than Wyoming is like Wisconsin. This is the rocky and mountainous province of Connaught—Galway, Mayo, Roscommon, Sligo and Leitrim are its counties—where dispossessed Irish Catholics were sent into exile after Oliver Cromwell turned their lands in Meath and Kildare over to English Protestants in the 17th Century. "Hell or Connaught" was the choice offered to them. But although the west is poor farming country—the fields under the purple mountain ranges are stony or swampy, bare, treeless and windswept—its Galway and Mayo seacoast, especially along the peninsula of Connemara, has some of the most spectacular scenic beauty in all of Europe, heightened by the region's atmosphere of unspoiled primitive simplicity and peacefulness that seems to detach it from the rest of the world.

Ireland in the west, the setting for some of John M. Synge's plays and William Butler Yeats's poems, looks more like the average American's misty-green, shamrock-bordered outdated picture postcard conception of the

In Island Isolation

Old Sod than do other parts of the country. Thatched cottage roofs, donkey carts and old women wrapped in long black shawls are fading from the midland and southern counties on the other side of the Shannon, but these reminders of bygone days are still seen along the narrow, stone-walled roads in Connaught and in the adjoining northern county of Donegal.

MOST housewives in Mayo and in the shadow of Connemara's dozen peaks, the Twelve Bens, still bake their bread in iron pots, with red coals of smoldering turf on top of the closed lid, and boil their bacon and cabbage in their cottages' fireplaces rather than on stoves. A fisherman putting out to sea from the nine-mile-long fiord of Killary Harbour, with the enormous walls of mountains more than 2,000 feet high rising out of the deep water beside him, rows an ancient type of tarred canvas boat called a currach. As his grandfathers did before him, he wears a sweater of white undyed wool, knitted in a distinctive design signifying his family name so that his body can be identified if he is drowned.

About 2,000 people, ignoring the jets from New York, London and Paris that zoom over their heads, persist in living as their ancestors did on the bleak rocks of the Aran Islands in the Atlantic off Galway Bay. They weave wool for their clothing, cure hides for their moccasin-like shoes and grow potatoes in crevices of the islands' solid limestone on thin patches of soil, carried in buckets from the mainland over past centuries or carefully nurtured by mixing beach sand and seaweed.

The old, poetic Gaelic language, dying elsewhere, is making its last stand in western Ireland. A statue of the famous roaming Gaelic storyteller, Padraic O Conaire, sitting on a pile of rocks like a little leprechaun, has been erected on the green in Galway's central square. Most of the offshore islanders do not speak English. Some years ago a group of them came to Belmullet, a small decayed seaport in Mayo, to watch the late Anew McMaster, the famed Irish actor, perform as Hamlet. They were

asked later if they were able to understand what McMaster was saying.

"Sure, we didn't understand it at all, but it was lovely to listen to," one of the island women said in Gaelic. "The words dripped off his tongue like cream."

A traveler driving south from Galway into Clare and Limerick on his way to Kerry begins to see an Ireland much different from the one he left behind. As always, he passes on the road farmers driving cattle and sheep to a village fair and wandering bands of tinkers, with their innumerable handsome red-headed children in horse-drawn caravan wagons. But at Ennis he finds new German-owned factories making carpets and sportswear, and a few miles farther on he comes to the vast new industrial complex beside the jet airport at Shannon, where British, German, American, Dutch, South African and Japanese companies, attracted by low labor costs and factory rentals and liberal tax concessions, are producing electronic equipment, machine parts, textiles, drilling materials, pianos, synthetic diamonds and transistor radios. A Shannon prospectus says to foreign investors: "In Ireland there is less danger of political upheaval than in any country in the world. Nowhere is the threat of extreme socialism or communism more remote." But an upheaval of another sort occurred recently at Shannon when the prize for excellence in the local national school's compulsory Gaelic language course was won by a little girl who is Japanese.

A YET more startling innovation awaits our traveler in Kerry. In the heart of that celebrated scenic wonderland, Killarney, a West German industrialist named Hans Liebherr has built a factory that makes cranes and excavating machinery. The same concern has also erected in the wild and rustic countryside near the Gap of Dunloe a shockingly modernistic hotel that bothers Irish people more than the crane factory.

The Kerrymen themselves, more practical than most of their countrymen, are inclined

TRICOLOR of green, white and orange is the Republic's flag.

GOLD HARP decorates Ireland's ancient green flag.

UNION JACK is the official emblem of the United Kingdom.

RED CROSS on a white field is the regional flag of Ulster.

THE FOUR BANNERS OF TWO ISLAND NEIGHBORS

The unions and divisions of Ireland are reflected in the four flags shown above. The tricolor at left, first flown in 19th Century rebellions against Britain, is intended to symbolize the melding of the island's people: green for the South, orange for the North. The flag next in line is older; the harp was an Irish instrument in very early times. The Union Jack, emblem of the United Kingdom of Great Britain, Scotland, Wales and Northern Ireland, carries the diagonal red cross of Saint Patrick superimposed upon the diagonal white cross of Saint Andrew, patron saint of Scotland, plus the right-angled red cross of Saint George of England—which is also seen on the Northern Ireland flag *(far right)*. The red hand in a white star recalls legends about the early conquest of Ireland; the royal crown symbolizes the British monarchy.

to take a tolerant view of this development. "Scenery is grand," one of them says, "but our young people can't live on it."

West German industry, bringing hope of stemming the tide of young Irish emigration, is more welcomed than the recent influx of West German farmers and retired businessmen who have been buying homes in western and southern Ireland. The Germans frankly admit that they are attracted by the Irish Government's steadfast neutrality and by the prevailing west wind, which they think less likely to carry nuclear fallout from Europe in the event of war. But they fence off the beaches of their newly acquired waterfront property, and this enrages the hospitable Irish. A wry joke, popular in Dublin, concerns a German settler in Kerry who has become so thoroughly Irish that his sons have gone off to work in England.

The famous scenery of Kerry, particularly in the lake district of Killarney, is different again from the rough and unruly rockiness of Connemara. Killarney is elegant and stately, with the blue water of its three lakes in a setting of rolling green lawns, forests of tall, graceful trees and massive growths of rhododendrons and other flowering shrubbery. It looks like a carefully landscaped great private estate, which, in fact, it is. Most of the lakeland is made up of the Muckross and Kenmare baronial domains, tended and trimmed over past centuries by battalions of gardeners and foresters.

But even the seacoast hills of Kerry, along Dingle Bay between Killorglin and Cahirciveen, where there are no trees at all, have a delicate refinement. Killorglin is the scene of the annual August Puck Fair, three days of merrymaking and cattle and horse trading when the pubs stay open nearly all night and a beribboned male goat presides as king of the festival on a platform in the market square. One explanation of this honoring of the goat is that, like many Irish ceremonies, it dates back hundreds of years to a battle against English invaders. A stampeding herd of goats gave warning of the enemy's approach and Killorglin has been expressing its gratitude ever since.

DOWN at the southern tip of the Kerry peninsula, overlooking the entrance to the River Kenmare, where smugglers' boats late in the 18th Century picked up Irish youths traveling secretly to Catholic seminaries in France and Spain, stands Darrynane, the home of Daniel O'Connell, the emancipator who "found the Irish peasants slaves and left them men." O'Connell's house was empty and falling into ruins until it was reconditioned by the government in 1967. But the young Irish Republic, for all its recent forward strides, has not yet been able to restore all its patriotic shrines. Kilmainham jail in Dublin, where the executed leaders of the 1916 Easter Week rebellion were imprisoned, was also decaying from neglect until a group of private citizens undertook to restore it with their own hands.

As he leaves the Kerry peninsula and resumes his exploration of the rest of Ireland—swinging from Cork across to the Irish Sea at Dublin and up that eastern shore into Ulster—the traveler becomes more aware that he is passing through a very old country, a place that was encrusted, long before Columbus discovered America, with the stony remains of many ages of civilization. To a stranger from Ohio, whose oldest settlement, Marietta, goes back only to 1788, the dates of even the more recent Irish monasteries, castles and towns seem incredible. The writers of the authoritative *Shell Guide to Ireland* mention casually, for example, that although "there were several churches and monasteries in the area in an early historic period, the story of Dublin as a city does not commence until A.D. 841."

TO an Irishman, this is not really old. At Newgrange in Meath, near Slane Hill where Saint Patrick lit his Paschal fire in 433, there is a Bronze Age burial chamber 4,000 years old. The whole country from Kerry to County Down in Ulster is scattered with prehistoric ring forts, druid stones and dolmens —large, flat rocks balanced on top of upright supporting boulders or slabs. They are thought to be either the altars of ancient sun worshipers or the inner walls of tombs once covered with earth. The capstone of one dolmen called the Giant's Grave at Kiltiernan, near Dublin, is 23 feet long, 17 feet wide and 6 feet thick. A farmer in the area doubts the theory that this enormous rock was lifted into place above its supporting stones by a hundred or more strong men straining in unison. "When could you get a hundred Irishmen to pull together?" he asks.

Relics of the early Christian era are all over Ireland: ancient Celtic crosses and the ruins of monastic settlements, like Clonmacnois on the Shannon in County Offaly where Saint Ciaran established a school for monks in 548, and where Rory O'Conor, the last High King of Ireland, was buried in 1198 after the Norman invasion. A small Sixth Century church, or oratory, looking like an overturned boat with its walls of corbeled stones arching to form a

pointed roof 14 feet high, stands remarkably intact on the Dingle peninsula. The countryside is dotted with the soaring round towers, some rising to 100 feet, where monks in the Ninth and Tenth Centuries climbed to escape the attacking Danes, pulling up the ladders behind them. Most of the towers are in a much better state of preservation than the surrounding churches and castles that were built hundreds of years later. Their limestone blocks are held firmly in place by a miraculous cement of the Middle Ages whose long-lost formula, the Irish say, contained cockleshells, egg whites, animal manure, ox blood and ox hair, lime, riverbed silt and sand.

But the most stirring ancient sight in all of Ireland is the mighty Rock of Cashel, stronghold of the Kings of Munster, rising high and abruptly over the surrounding green plains of Tipperary. Crowning the heights of the steep rock, where Saint Patrick baptized a King of Munster in 450, are the great gray walls of a 13th Century cathedral and its adjoining archbishop's castle, a 10th Century round tower and Cormac MacCarthy's gem-perfect little Romanesque chapel, built in 1134, which ranks beside the beautifully illuminated Eighth Century *Book of Kells* as one of Ireland's proudest inheritances from its golden Middle Ages.

AERIAL photographs of the rock show that the walls of the cathedral and the older chapel, crowding closely on each other, are built on slightly diverging lines. The chapel was dedicated to Mary. It was oriented on a point of the compass a few degrees north of east so that the rising sun in May, the month of Mary, would shine directly into its altar window, while the cathedral, dedicated to Saint Patrick, was built to face the sun on the morning of the 17th of March.

Ireland's history is divided sharply by the Anglo-Norman invasion of 1170, which separates the earlier golden centuries when the nation, under its own High Kings, was a flourishing center of ecclesiastical learning, from the later 700-odd years of subjugation under the English. Cashel represents the old Celtic Ireland. It was established as a royal fortress in 370, and after the country was converted, the rock was ruled by leaders who were bishops as well as kings. They produced such works as the *Book of Rights,* a code of laws composed in Gaelic verse. Irishmen like to point out the contrast between the exquisite artistry of Cormac's pre-Norman chapel and the heavy grayness of the Anglo-Norman cathedral built beside it in the rock's later, declining years.

THE early Celtic Irish did not congregate in towns; they were farmers and herdsmen whose only built-up settlements were monastic communities, like Clonmacnois, or forts, like Cashel. The handsome castles of Irish feudal estates and the lovely cathedral towns came with the Normans, who also developed the small Scandinavian seaport bases at Dublin, Cork and Limerick into medieval cities. The traveler today finds those three Irish cities, along with Belfast, each as different from the others as are the east, south, west and north parts of the country where they are respectively located.

Belfast is the least Irish; when the other four fifths of Ireland broke away from the United Kingdom in 1921, Belfast became the capital of the six northern Ulster counties that remained loyal to London because they had little in common with the rebels. It is the only Irish city that is Protestant rather than Roman Catholic (many of Belfast's playgrounds, and all of its pubs, are closed on Sunday) and the only one affected by the Industrial Revolution of the 19th Century, which boomed its shipbuilding and textile manufacturing and raised its heavily Scottish population from 25,000 to 350,000 in that period. With its long rows of grimy laborers' houses, Belfast has the very un-Irish look of a hard-worked factory town.

There is little sternness, however, in the look of the pretty Ulster coastal country. The tourist who ventures into this northeast corner of Ireland, seldom mentioned by the travel articles that praise Kerry and Galway, finds himself in a vacation land of green mountains and long sandy beaches, crowded during the summer holidays with visitors from Britain and Scotland who sail, golf and cycle and bowl on outdoor greens. This is the country where Finn MacCool, the legendary Irish hero, scooped up a vast piece of sod, thereby creating the lake of Lough Neagh, and hurled the sod into the Irish Sea to form the Isle of Man. The Antrim Coast Road, running along the edge of the water beside the hills and brightly colored glens of the Antrim Mountains north of Belfast, has views as stunning as those along the Adriatic coast of Italy.

The industrialized North of Ireland, with its new plants which are envied in Dublin, stands as aloof as ever from the Republic. The gulf may be narrowing, but religious differences are still strongly felt. On July 12, Orangeman's Day, the city streets and country roads of Ulster are draped with colorful banners proclaiming allegiance to the Queen, and back-alley fences are chalked with antipapist slogans.

AN American tourist picked up two teenaged hitchhikers recently near a small temporary bridge on the Ulster border. "What happened to the bridge?" he asked.

"Blown up by them men that blow up the bridges."

"And what men are they?"

The boy eyed the stranger carefully and said, "Don't they call them the I.R.A.?"

The underground Irish Republican Army, which fought the British to win freedom for Ireland and which has never accepted the separateness of Ulster, was officially disbanded by its old leader, President Eamon de Valera. But it is yet alive, although nonviolent and dwindling in numbers. When riots broke out in Northern Ireland in the summer of 1969, Northern I.R.A. leaders received no arms support from Dublin's I.R.A., which wants to bring back the partitioned six counties by political means rather than by force.

Cork is the Irish Naples, the throbbing and lively city of the south. It was the hotbed of the revolution. Its main business district, City Hall and public library were burned in 1920 by British constabulary troops. When a peace-seeking priest in Cork talked against the rebellion, the men and women rose and quietly walked out of the church—returning after the sermon, of course, for the consecration and communion. Resentment against the partition, somewhat softened elsewhere by pleas for tolerance from de Valera, remains strong in Cork and in the smaller provincial western city of Limerick. A crowd of some 30,000 people gathered in Limerick a few years ago for the funeral of an I.R.A. youth named Sean South who was killed during a foray into Ulster.

THE capital city of Dublin, the only place in the Republic with traffic and parking problems, is less concerned with old political sores than with present economic needs. To picture Dublin, imagine an old city, rather threadbare, whose public buildings and town houses were built by wealthy aristocrats in the elegant Georgian period before the American Revolution. Like all of Ireland, Dublin was tired and battered from the invasions of Cromwell and William of Orange when it was taken over in the 18th Century by a new ruling class of Protestant landowners known as the Anglo-Irish ascendancy, who moved into the city to run the Irish Parliament in its magnificent new building on College Green.

These titled grandees, reveling in their sudden rise to national leadership, hired the best architects and building craftsmen of the day to create an Irish capital city suitably splendid for their cultured taste. During their reign they built the superbly designed Custom House on the River Liffey, Trinity College campus, the Four Courts and all of Dublin's palatial private residences, including the Leinster House—said to be a prototype for the later United States White House. Then in 1800, when prosperous Dublin was spreading in all directions, the Act of Union dissolved Ireland's Parliament and moved its legislature, like those of Wales and Scotland, to London. The boom in Dublin

collapsed and the city came to a standstill. It has not changed much since.

Parts of O'Connell Street, the main Dublin thoroughfare, had to be rebuilt after they were demolished by artillery fire in the 1916 rebellion, but the heart of Dublin, with no skyscrapers and no express highways, remains as it was in the 18th Century when Jonathan Swift was Dean of Saint Patrick's Cathedral. The old Parliament House, with its rounded front of stately gray-white columns, houses the Bank of Ireland. The fine houses of the earls and knights stand undisturbed on Merrion Square, even if they are occupied now by Government agencies and by business and professional firms. Other Georgian homes are falling into shabby neglect in poor neighborhoods, but antiquarian committees are now fighting to keep them from being torn down.

"Ireland is the only civilized-looking country left in Europe," one of the Georgian-house defenders says. "We must keep it that way."

But Ireland, with its roadside directional signs stubbornly printed in Gaelic, finds it increasingly hard to cling to the charms of the past. The country's age-old need—more better-paid work to keep young Irishmen from emigrating—continues to be one of Ireland's most pressing problems. A frightening average of 30,000 or more Irish people, mostly young, emigrated each year in recent decades.

POLITICAL freedom, after long centuries of dreaming of it and fighting for it, came as a letdown to Ireland. Olivia Robertson, a discerning observer of the Irish character, has compared modern Ireland to a man who has been proposing gallantly for years to an unresponsive woman—and then finds himself unexpectedly accepted. He has never really thought much about what marriage would be like. Now he has a wife and family to support and not much money with which to pay the rent.

The problems brought on by independence were difficult ones, and only today is Ireland getting over the shock of discovering that realization is not as rosy as expectation.

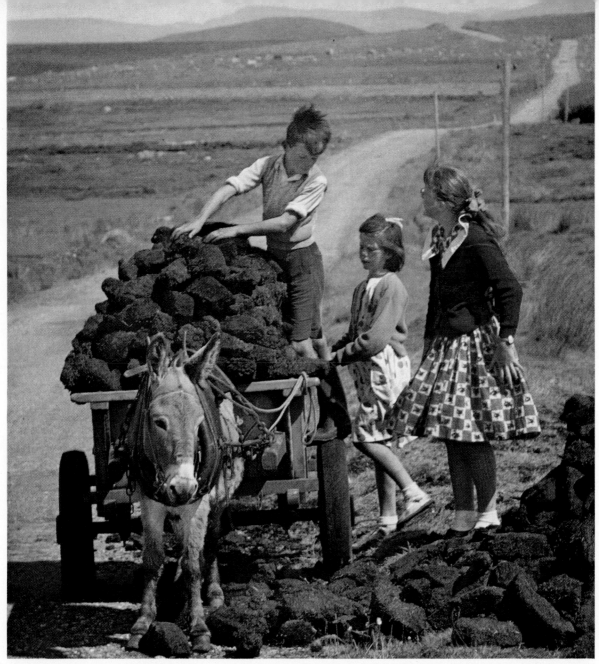

As their donkey waits, children of County Mayo load a cart with peat before taking the sunlit road leading to their home town.

A Quiet Setting for Yesterday's Eventful Dramas

Much of Ireland is sparsely settled today. In the countryside the long, peaceful perspectives are only occasionally broken by the figures of children playing or farm people going about their tasks. The quiet is in a way misleading: the loneliness speaks of centuries of pain and violence. Nothing of the past has been forgotten; the very names of the hills and towns conjure up remembrances of battles and famine. Although at first glance the landscape appears to be solitary and untouched, closer inspection reveals that every valley, crag and field has been marked by human hands. Even the most blissful pasture, buzzing with sounds of summer, is redolent of bitter memories of war, hunger and emigration. The island's past crowds thickly about every slope.

17

AN ISOLATED COTTAGE in County Donegal in the northwest is crossed by shifting cloud patterns of light and dark. The simple construction, employing whitewashed walls and thatched roof, is typical of Ireland's west. Although the mountains and jagged coastline of Donegal are barren, the valleys are fertile areas for growing flax and raising sheep.

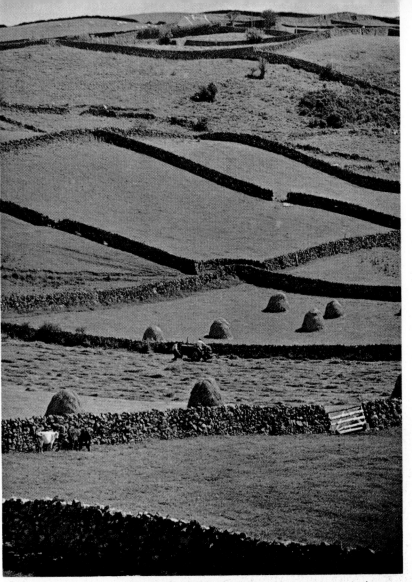

SEQUESTERED FIELDS, separated into neat rectangles by stone walls, provide a Galway farmer with hay and pasturage. The hilliest part of the land *(background)* is too steep to cultivate.

TROUT FISHING absorbs the attention of a father and his sons in Connemara, County Galway's lake district. In the distance rises the series of peaks known as the Twelve Bens.

Collecting supplies, a group of Aran Islanders moves from shore in a currach, a type of vessel made of wood and tarred canvas in use

for more than 1,500 years. It is as primitive as life in the Islands, one of the last places where Gaelic is still an everyday language.

JUTTING into the sea, Dingle peninsula in County Kerry *(opposite)* is the mainland's westernmost part. Because arable land is scarce in the west, fields are planted to the cliff's edge.

GRAZING on upland pastures, powerful workhorses roam the Sheeffry hills in County Mayo. Since the 1846 potato famine, pastoral farming has superseded crop growing in importance.

EVENING PERSPECTIVE of Londonderry, an old seaport in Northern Ireland, reveals rich grain fields which roll right to the edge of the suburbs hard by the peaceful River Foyle.

GEORGIAN SYMMETRY of St. Stephen's Protestant Church in Dublin and the formal façades of town houses along Upper Mount Street recall the days of the Anglo-Irish aristocracy.

2

An Elusive, Unmistakable Character

IT is often said that Ireland's most outstanding export is people. Just as often it is observed that descendants of Irish immigrants removed from Ireland for as many as three generations, like John Fitzgerald Kennedy, remain labeled as Irish. "I was born in the United States and so was my father before me but my children are still called Irish," Kennedy's father once protested. "What the hell do we have to do to become Americans?"

In a perceptive study of the question, the British essayist V. S. Pritchett decided that the Irish preserve their singularity in lands other than their own because they constitute a great world-wide secret society, dedicated to protecting their racial imagination. It may be more simply that the Irish stand apart from long force of habit; after centuries of resisting assimilation by the British at home, they are now slow to accept it abroad. But whatever the cause, clannishness—like that of the Kennedy family—is the deepest trait of the Irish and many of their other characteristics stem from it.

Togetherness is carried to extremes in Ireland. Despite its good Atlantic harbors, the country lacks a sizable fishing industry or a substantial commercial maritime fleet largely because Irishmen refuse to stay away from home overnight. In the west of Ireland, *bon voyage* parties for young people emigrating to America or going off to work in England are called "wakes" because they are as sad as burials. Weddings are often heartbreaking ordeals for the families involved. A foreign visitor in Dublin recently noticed a young woman in traveling clothes standing alone in front of a hotel while three men were weeping bitterly with their arms around each other in the hotel doorway.

"It's just a wedding," a passerby explained. "That's the bride and there's the groom saying goodbye to his father and his grandfather."

SUCH intense devotion to parents has been as responsible as economic strain and emigration for Ireland's notoriously delayed marriages and its high population of bachelors and spinsters. Before performing a wedding ceremony in Roscommon a few years ago, the village priest had to read up on the ritual because he had long forgotten it. All over Ireland, long-engaged couples have waited for a mother or father to die before getting married. There was always the son who stayed at home to run the farm for his aging parents, and he hesitated to disturb the authority of his mother by bringing a wife into the house. For the Irish to put love and romance before family obligation violated age-old traditions. But urbanization and industrialization are freeing young people from their close ties to home. Emigration is decreasing as more jobs are becoming available. The number of marriages has been rising and the marriage age declining. Old social patterns are beginning to break down.

Yet the attachment between an Irish mother and her son has remained strong. The father is the head of the closely knit family and he takes charge of the boys when they reach the age of seven or eight. In many Irish country homes, as in the farm belt of the American Midwest and in Japan, the housewife does not eat dinner until the men have left the table. She has no part in her husband's social life; he goes off with his sons and other men to the village pub and to

football and hurling matches while she stays home with her daughters. In small-town churches, the men and boys sit separately from women and girls at Sunday Mass.

But within the family circle, the mother has the prestige and influence of a queen, and she intercedes powerfully for her son in disputes between him and his father. She sees to it that her son gets the best cut of the meat, sometimes better than the one she serves to her husband. She secretly slips him money for a dance. She hates the thought of his leaving home to marry, and in many cases, so does he.

The bonds of an Irish family are deep between brothers and sisters and their uncles, aunts and grandparents. A courageous bride who does venture into a home with parents-in-law is likely to find herself also caring for her husband's widowed aunt and elderly grandfather and perhaps his 50-year-old bachelor brother. It is a disgrace for a family to let old relatives live alone and a scandalous shame to put a granduncle or an aged aunt among strangers in a nursing home or public institution.

THE loyalty of an Irishman to his brother is illustrated by a conversation between two farmers in a pub at Dunaff in Donegal. One of the men said that he knew somebody who could leap 15 feet backwards. "That's a physical impossibility," the other man said. "There isn't a human being on this earth capable of performing such a feat. I'm surprised that you should stand there and expect me to swallow such a desperate falsehood. Now tell me, will you not, who did you ever see jump backwards 15 feet?"

"Your own brother Dinny."

"My brother Dinny? Aye, sure, of course, Dinny could do it. Many's the time I've seen Dinny give a jump backwards not only 15 feet but sometimes 20 and 23 feet."

A priest in Kilkenny, now in his 70s, has been harboring a resentment against an older brother in New York for more than 50 years because of what he considers an inexcusable breach of family loyalty: "When he left home to go to America, he promised me on his knees that he would come back for my ordination as a priest three years later. He never came. Don't tell me it might have been hard for him to make the trip. Our poor old Aunt Mary made it, traveling alone all the way from St. Paul, Minnesota."

AS warmly cheerful and charming as they are, the Irish self-consciously hide their deep emotions beneath a careful composure for appearances' sake. "There's no kissing in public in this country and none at home either if the children are present," an Irishwoman says. But their upright propriety melts into helpless anguish when death takes away a member of the family. At a funeral in Cork a middle-aged man cried out as the coffin was carried from the church, "Oh, Gran-da! Gran-da! You're dead and gone! Who'll jam me bread now?" At wakes in Galway and Sligo, women relatives and neighbors spell each other during the night "keening," wailing Gaelic ejaculations of grief for the dead like those in the dialogue of Synge's *Riders to the Sea.* ("He's gone now, God spare us, and we'll not see him again. He's gone now, and when the black night is falling I'll have no son left in the world.")

However, the old traditional Irish wake, with several nights of drinking and storytelling, is now only a remembrance of the past. Long discouraged by the Church because of its pagan rites, mock-marriages and anticlerical joking, the custom was brought to an end by 20th-Century burial practices and the spread of the English language.

The present procedure is to wake the body for only one night at home. Then it is taken to the church, where there is a brief service with a rosary on the second evening, with the funeral on the following morning. The Irish funeral is an important event in the community, attended by people from surrounding counties and reported at length in the local newspaper with paragraphs of lavish praise for the dead person. ("Deeply devoted to his family, he took a passionate interest in their happiness and well being.") Sometimes, in keeping with the customs of older generations, a group of friends will come forward after the Requiem Mass to dismiss the hearse and carry the coffin from the church to the cemetery on their shoulders.

Their staunch respect for parental authority, along with their acceptance of the moral doctrines of the Roman Catholic Church, has made the Irish law-abiding, conventional and conservative. There is little crime in Ireland. Women feel at ease alone on the Dublin streets late at night, and it is common to see respectable matrons hitchhiking on country roads. An elderly lady who lives alone on the main street of a midland town leaves the key inserted on the outside of her front door's spring lock day and night so that callers can enter without summoning her from the kitchen. Dublin and Belfast have their quota of gum-chewing and twisting teenaged girls with teased hair and tight skirts, and boys with sideburns and narrow, sharply pointed shoes, but Ireland has no juvenile delinquency worth mentioning—and no night life after its bars close at 11:30.

The inborn esteem of the Irish for moral law and authority enables them to submit to Government restrictions that would outrage liberals in other Western democracies. The constitution of the Republic, drawn up by Eamon de Valera in 1936, forbids divorce and provides for a censorship that has banned even the books of Graham Greene and other Catholic novelists, and forced them to be sold under the counter in Dublin. It is illegal for an Irish druggist to sell any kind of contraceptive device. The lurid big-circulation British Sunday newspapers are required to remove racy sex stories from editions sent to Ireland.

A CHAMPION of individual rights and freedom who tried to change these laws, moreover, would find many of the Irish against him. "You must remember that this Constitution was drawn to suit the Irish people, who are very strict in matters of morals," wrote the late Robert Briscoe, the Jewish sometime Lord Mayor of Dublin, in his memoirs, *For the Life of Me.*

"It is generally considered that the Puritans of America were the most uncompromising moralists of all time and that Roman Catholics are distinctly flexible in this respect. I assure you this only applies to Catholics in Latin countries. The Irish Catholic is as puritanical as any passenger on the *Mayflower* and de Valera is notably straight-laced. Indeed for purity of mind and rectitude of conduct he would make Elder Brewster seem a libertine." But in the late 1960s the constitution's restrictive sections, including the one on divorce, came increasingly under attack. Some Irishmen thought the constitution should be revised *in toto*. Legislation was even enacted that automatically "unbans" any banned book after ten years.

DISCUSSING the moral code of the Irish, Briscoe recalled the civil war in 1922 when, as one of de Valera's Republicans, his name was placed on a list of enemies whom Free State soldiers were to shoot on sight. Walking unarmed one day in Dublin, he came upon a Free State officer, Sean MacEoin, who recognized him and drew a gun. Briscoe turned his back on MacEoin and walked safely away.

"I was sure that no Irishman like MacEoin would shoot anybody in the back and I was right," Briscoe said. He added that whenever he saw Sean he thanked him and that Sean loudly cursed the high principles that kept him from pulling the trigger.

Ireland's stern moral standards, more repressive in the small country towns than in the cities, have prompted many restless young people to move to England; they are as anxious for excitement as for better-paying jobs. "As teen-agers, my sisters and I would walk a mile from our house to the main road, just to sit on a wall and watch the motorcars drive by," says a young woman who grew up on a farm in County Limerick. "And some evenings there weren't many motorcars."

Puritanical though they may be, the Irish take a quite tolerant view of what other nations have long regarded the island's most conspicuous moral problem, the Irishman's proverbial "weakness for the drink." The Irish-born playwright George Bernard Shaw, among others, has suggested that the Irishman finds his imagination too tortuous to bear without whiskey. The Irish deny this allegation. They point out that habitual drinkers in Ireland vastly prefer the country's black Guinness stout and lager beer to whiskey, and that these brews are not the drink of a tormented alcoholic. They blame modern Irish literature and literary biography, so filled with figures like James Joyce's father, lifting a convivial glass with friends in a pub while his family is being evicted, for making the singing alcoholic almost as much a symbol of Ireland in non-Irish minds as the shamrock and the shillelagh.

The average Irishman sees nothing especially deplorable in the fact that a village like Milltown Malbay in County Clare, with a population of 650 people, has 27 licensed pubs, or public bars. The pub plays an important role in Irish social life. Unlike an American, the Irishman seldom drinks at home except on special festive occasions—partly because his wife, like most middle-class Irishwomen, is likely to be a teetotaler. He prefers having his glass of stout in the male company that he finds in a pub, and so he spends an hour or two there in the evening.

SMALL villages with only one or two butcher shops or tobacco and candy stores will have several pubs because there are different types to suit different male tastes. Some are noisy, filled with songs and jovial chatter, and others are quiet and dignified. The pub-going habit in Ireland is not confined to the working class as it is in Britain. Many wealthy socialites, who live in large, servant-staffed country homes —and whose wives join them in a drink—spend an hour before dinner with their friends in a village pub.

"It's much more entertaining than sitting by ourselves in the living room at home," the wife of a millionaire horse breeder in County Meath says. "In the pub, we hear all the local news and gossip. Then we go to our homes for dinner. Sometimes we return to the pub later for a nightcap. We Irish feel that drinking alone at home is dull and antisocial.''

The Irish distaste for drinking in the quiet of the home used to make the annual St. Patrick's Day dog show in Dublin one of the year's most popular sporting events. Until the law was changed a few years ago, pubs were closed on St. Patrick's Day, a holy day in Ireland, but one bar at the dog show was allowed to stay open during that event. Consequently the show was stormed by crowds of non-dog lovers from all over Dublin. One year Brendan Behan, fighting the crush around the bar, stepped on the paw of a terrier on its way to the judging circle. The burly dramatist glared at the contestant's owner and said, "Now isn't this a silly place to bring a dog?''

DURING a discussion of the function of the Irish pub, a Dubliner cited a memorable line spoken by Barry Fitzgerald in *The Quiet Man*, the Academy Award-winning movie comedy of Irish country life directed by John Ford. Fitzgerald, on his way to a pub, declares, ''I think I'll go and join me comrades and talk a little treason.''

''The fellow who wrote that line knew Ireland,'' the Dubliner said. ''He makes his character out to be heading for the pub not so much because he wants a drink but mainly because he wants to talk before an audience. That's the Irish pub, a stage for the orator, and that's an Irishman—a performer who loves to hear himself talk. Treason, of course, is now out as a timely topic of discourse because Ireland, sad to say, has won her political freedom, leaving a great yawning gap in his repertoire, but he finds enough other things to talk about until the bartender shuts off the lights and pushes him into the street.''

The long conversations in Ireland are not confined to the atmosphere of pubs or to men; they go on everywhere at all hours between people of both sexes and all ages. In the morning, hauling his wagon of milk cans from the creamery, the farmer stops his tractor in

IRELAND'S COUNTIES have special importance. Although their political significance is slight, they receive strong emotional allegiance from their inhabitants, and this is true also in Great Britain's six Northern counties *(dark shading)* which are commonly known as Ulster. The other provinces, holdovers of Ireland's ancient kingdoms, are much less vital in Irish life.

the road, turns off the motor, and listens, leaning on the steering wheel, while a neighbor woman talks to him from her cottage doorway. Two small, red-cheeked boys, with their books in leather cases strapped on their backs like soldiers' knapsacks, talk wildly all the way home from school. A girl of 20, in a coat of the bright royal blue that seems to be the Irishwoman's favorite color, leans out of a window in the Limerick-Dublin bus while it is stopped in Monasterevin, beckons to a young man standing nearby and chatters to him, smiling and laughing. A Frenchman or a Welshman might misunderstand her intentions, but the Irish youth knows that she is talking only to pass the time until the bus starts moving again.

The stage Irishman is said to be a cliché of fiction, but Ireland is full of sly Barry Fitzgeralds and crisp, swaggering James Cagneys, and every neighborhood has its Brendan Behan, eager to confide a few thousand choice words that just occurred to him. The Irish fondle a word and rub it and polish it before carefully arranging it in a sentence. "In these beautiful mountains, heaven is a foot and a half above the height of a man," a Kerrywoman says. A priest watches an elderly and ailing parishioner hobbling weakly from the church and says, "He's walking slow but he's going fast." An old man in a crowded pub holds up a pint glass of Guinness and says, "If this be a ghost that I see here in my hand before me, I hope it reappears again soon." Pritchett, in his essay on the Irish character, tells of seeing a huge political sign, "Vote for Duffey," on a wall near Dublin and next to it, added by the opposition in letters running for more than a hundred yards, "And Ireland's dead will rise and curse you."

Two strangers carry on a conversation in a hotel dining room with a white-haired, red-faced Irishman seated alone at a nearby table. When they leave, one says that it was a pleasure to talk with him.

"I would say the same to you, sir," the elderly Irishman replies, "but it would sound repetitive."

THE Gaelic wit shines in sharp retorts and deflating sarcasm. Asked if the cream is fresh, a waitress says, "If it was any fresher, it would be grass." A street-corner loafer eyes the brand new pigskin gloves of a lucky companion who has made a big killing at the races and remarks sneeringly, "Isn't it curious that when a man comes into wealth, suddenly his hands get cold?" An auctioneer named McGrath, trying to sell a black iron cooking pot, spots the town's Protestant minister in the audience and yells at him, "Now this nice round little pot would make a lovely bell for your church."

"With your tongue in it, Mr. McGrath?" the minister says.

A Canadian who lives in Dublin is dissatisfied with the education his children are receiving in their Irish national elementary school; they are taught, he says, too much by rote and memory drilling. But the talk of Irish laborers and farmers and young errand boys and shop girls, with only a few years of such education, displays an erudition and command of language that astonishes foreigners today as it astonished William Makepeace Thackeray in Cork in 1842. ("I listened to two boys almost in rags: they were lolling over the quay balustrade, and talking about *one of the Ptolemys!* and talking very well, too . . . with a great deal of fire and eloquence.") Today a cabdriver in Cork recites Robert Burns, not in modern schoolbook English, but in Burns's original difficult Scottish-Gaelic dialect. Kathleen Cavanagh, proprietress of a vegetable shop in the gray medieval town of Birr, lectures to a visitor on the Brehon Laws of early Celtic Ireland, pausing now and then to urge a customer to try the new Duke of York potatoes.

THE clannishness of the Irish brought on an intense wave of nationalism when the old Free State won self-government from the British in 1921. Only now, under economic need for foreign friendships and the passing of the older revolutionists, is that aloofness wearing thin. One less-than-successful effort to bring back the glory of ancient independent Ireland was de Valera's struggle to revive the Gaelic language, the tongue spoken by the Irish Catholic peasants until 150 years ago.

The constitution drawn up in 1936 declared Gaelic to be the national and "first official" language, and it became a compulsory subject in the schools. An earlier Gaelic revival movement, which coincided with the beginnings of the Irish drive for independence, had been warmly welcomed by the Irish people because it was a gesture of defiance against the British. But after the British were gone, the realistic Irish saw little to be gained from speaking a language understood by nobody else in the shrinking modern world. Besides, Gaelic is difficult for English-speaking Irish to master. Its alphabet is strange and its words have letters that are not pronounced: Dun Laoghaire, the Gaelic name for the town of Dunleary, is pronounced "Doon Laye-reh." The official Gaelic title for the Irish Prime Minister, *Taoiseach,* is sounded "tea-shock."

WITH characteristic Irish stubbornness, de Valera persisted in pushing the old language while he was heading the Government in the 1930s and 1940s. If two doctors applied for a public health office, the appointment would go automatically to the one who spoke Gaelic, even if his qualifications were inferior. School children were given extra credit in history or geography examinations if their papers were written in Gaelic. Gaelic scholars like Frank O'Connor, a leading Irish writer, were amused by the Government's attempts to put Gaelic names on things like the Irish Hospital Sweepstakes lottery, which became, in literal Gaelic, The Little Sweeping Brushes of the Hospitals of Ireland.

Gaelic is still required in the schools but Sean Lemass, who succeeded de Valera as the Prime Minister in 1959, indicated that he was far more concerned about Ireland's economic future than its linguistic heritage; he was not anxious to put a language barrier in the way of foreign investors who were bringing industry into the country. So the Gaelic revival, never very strong, quickly began to dwindle. Only in parts of the west coast, where English was never spoken, is Gaelic still used in daily conversation. It is now hard to believe that as late as 1541, when Henry VIII had himself named King of Ireland—because "the Irish have the foolish opinion that the Bishop of Rome is King of Ireland"—the proclamation had to be translated into Gaelic so that the Irish peers in the Dublin Parliament could understand it.

But Ireland's attachment to the past is so strong that even young people, who admit that the speaking of Gaelic is ridiculously impractical, hate to see their old language go. "When you go to Galway and hear people speaking Irish, you feel deeply ashamed of yourself for not understanding what they're saying," one Dublin youth says.

The Republic of Ireland, of course, is the only English-speaking country that is Roman Catholic. And within the worldwide Catholic Church, it stands apart from other Catholic countries because of the special burning zeal that shines in the Irish people's faith. The Irishman can never be as casual and relaxed in his religious belief as a devout French, Italian or English Catholic can be; he is too seriously and anxiously concerned with the hereafter. One of the recent Italian Popes is said to have remarked, "Isn't Irish Catholicism a terrifying thing?"

Worship in Ireland is not postponed until Sunday. Many families kneel together every evening to say the rosary at home, and there are people in the churches at all hours attending novenas, benediction, and special spiritual retreat and mission services, making the stations of the cross or merely paying a quick visit to light a holy candle. The Church is the one thing that comes before obligations to the beloved family. The mother who is reluctant to see her son married will never raise her voice in protest if he decides to go off to Africa as a missionary for the rest of his life. Yet with all this constant devotion, Irish men and women are always possessed with the feeling that they are not doing enough for God.

STRIVING for extra gifts of grace, they are continually making pilgrimages and other special acts of penance and sacrifice. More than a half million Irish wear the Sacred Heart pin of the Pioneers, which means that, purely as a religious offering of self-denial, they have made a vow never to take an alcoholic drink. The Pioneers are not reformed drinkers; most of them took their pledge in childhood, or in their early teens, and have never tasted alcohol.

Anybody who tries to analyze the Irish character finds himself confronted with baffling contradictions. With all their intense religious devotion the Irish are superstitious people, believers in ghosts and fairies and good luck charms. A mother who hears her son's good looks praised by a visitor hastens to sew a small bag of salt to the child's coat to protect him from being stolen by "the little people."

"I don't believe in them," an Irishman will say about fairies, "but they are there."

Despite their ready supplies of wit and humor, the Irish are quick to take offense when they are laughed at, and for all their pride in their countrymen's accomplishments, they acknowledge a large amount of truth in Samuel Johnson's often-quoted observation: "The Irish are a fair people; they never speak well of one another." ("He's made a brilliant success as a surgeon in Dublin, but I've been told he never sends a penny to his poor old sick uncle over in Ballacolla.") The Irish are famous for their warm hospitality: soup and a steak are put before a visitor at 10:30 at night despite his protests that he has already had dinner. But as one student of the Irish personality has written, in such a small country where gossip travels fast, hospitality is not only a virtue; it can also be a precaution. The housewife may be afraid that someone will say of her, "She never asked me if I had a mouth on me."

THE Irish are given to sudden and perverse moods of suspicion or flaring anger. Ireland itself, much to its surprise, was declared a republic in 1948 through a fit of temper.

Until that time, under the leadership of de Valera, Ireland had retained association with the British Commonwealth as a self-governing free state. Although he wanted Ireland to become a republic eventually, de Valera felt that a complete break from the Commonwealth would wipe away any remaining hope of recovering the six partitioned Irish counties of the North that had remained part of the United Kingdom in 1921.

In 1948 de Valera's Fianna Fail Party lost control of Parliament. The opposition leader, John A. Costello, became Prime Minister in a coalition government. After he took office, Costello went to Canada to take part in a Commonwealth bar association conference. The conference members were entertained one evening by the Governor General of Canada, Field Marshal Earl Alexander of Tunis. Alexander is a northern Irish Protestant, born in County Tyrone, the son of an earl with little sympathy for the Catholic rebels of the south. He did not speak to Costello.

Leaving the dinner in a rage, Costello immediately summoned reporters and announced that he was breaking all ties with the British Commonwealth—and therefore, of course, with Northern Ireland—and that he would make Ireland an independent republic.

THE Prime Minister's abrupt announcement left the Irish in Dublin open-mouthed with astonishment. His own party, the Fine Gael, had been advocating a closer union with the Commonwealth. His opposition, de Valera's Nationalists, who had fought for a republic in the civil war, were in no position to object to Costello's proposal, but privately the status of a republic, erecting a higher barrier between them and the six Northern counties, was the last thing they wanted. But having publicly committed himself, Costello had no choice but to put a bill before the Irish Parliament asking for a republic.

"The Dail ratified Costello's unilateral declaration," wrote Robert Briscoe, a member of the legislature at that time. "We had to. He had made us look foolish enough in the eyes of the world without the stupidity of disavowing our Prime Minister. . . . But the timing of it and the manner of it can only be put down to personal pique."

And so it was that the Republic of Ireland, the dream of the Irish for centuries, finally came into being at a time when nobody particularly wanted it—because of an Irishman's unpredictable personality.

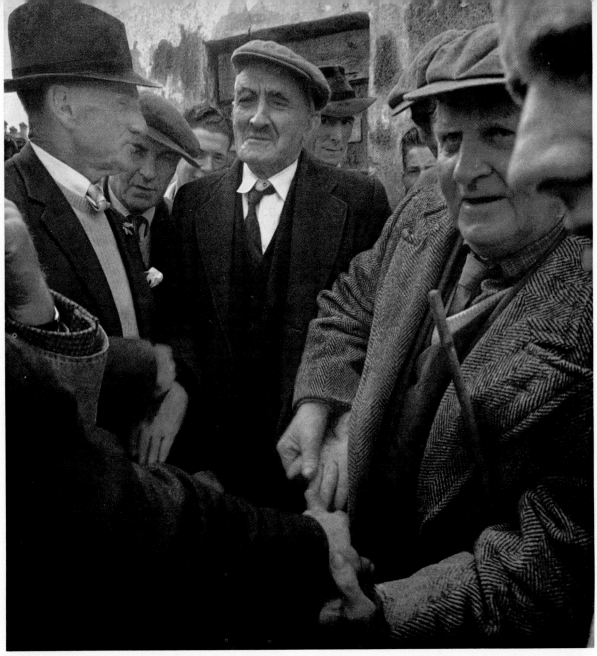

Concluding hours of horse bargaining, the buyer and seller join hands with a go-between at Puck Fair in Killorglin, County Kerry.

An Expressiveness Attuned to Whimsy and Wit

One way to gauge the temperament of a nation is to listen to its talk. The Irish personality is not in the words themselves but in the tone of voice. Hyperboles are delivered with a guileless inflection; wondrous events are related with hushed admiration; foolishness is crushed with the laconic sting of a question. Each individual cultivates his own style of conversation, and each region has its verbal idiosyncrasies. Yet wherever words are exchanged, whether between two cronies in a pub, a priest and a penitent in confession, or a mother and son in their hillside cottage, the language exposes quick imagination and wide-ranging association of thought. The Irish tongue records every nuance of a rich fancy.

*PILGRIMS annually ascend
a gaunt peak to honor Saint Patrick's
trials and good works*

AT THE SUMMIT of the mountain, Croagh Patrick in County Mayo, thousands of the devout, some of them barefoot, wait to hear sermons in Gaelic and English on the last Sunday of July.

ON THE TRAIL that reputedly traces Saint Patrick's ascent during his 40-day fast in 441 A.D., Catholics climb the 2,510-foot height, stopping to perform the traditional stations.

BEFORE AN ORATORY built in 1905 on the site of a ruined mountain-top shrine, Communion is offered at dawn. The annual pilgrimage draws priests and laymen from all over the world.

A LONELY INDEPENDENCE *is still the rule in remote regions of the land*

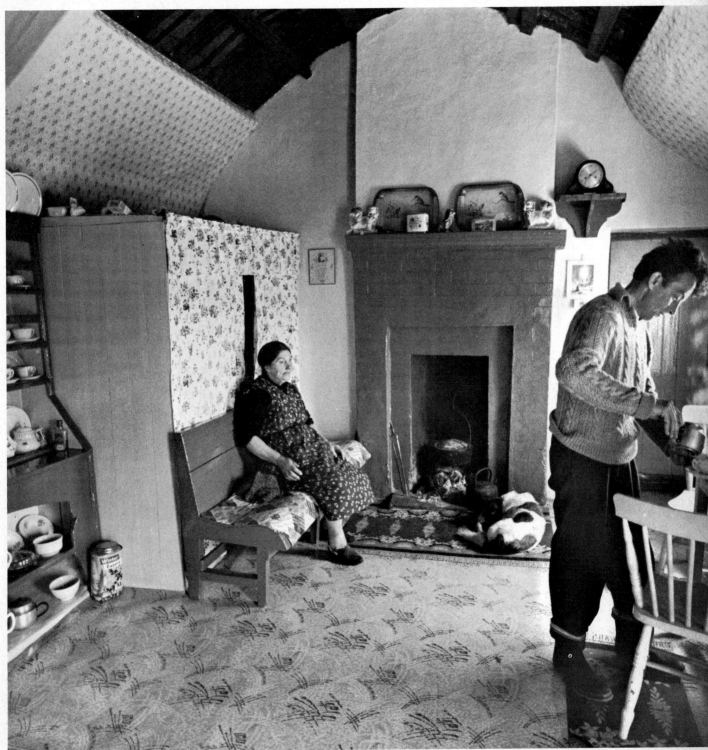

WHITEWASHED COTTAGE of three small rooms on one level *(opposite)* is the home of Mrs. Mary Sharkey in County Donegal. Her son Patrick repairs the thatched roof while she knits.

SPOTLESS INTERIOR is heated by a peat-burning fireplace and oven. As Patrick pours himself a cup of tea, Mrs. Sharkey sits by the curtained alcove which serves as her bedroom.

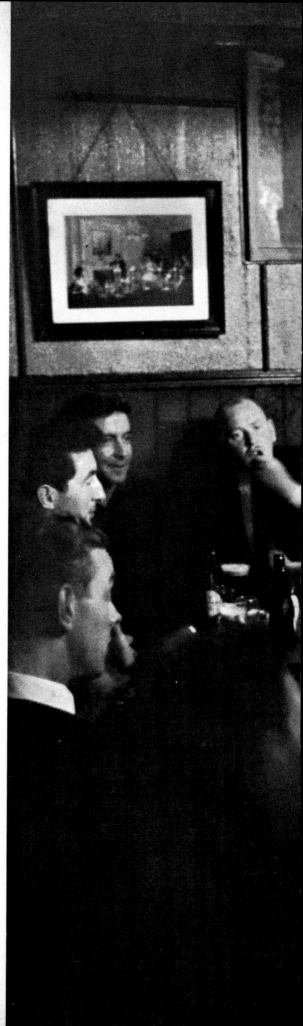

ROUSING CHORUS is raised by a circle of singing Ulstermen in the Cuan Bar, a pub in Strangford, County Down. The singers hold glasses of stout, which is the favorite Irish drink.

IMPASSIONED SPEECH captivates regulars at Dublin's The Brazen Head as it would have in the late 18th Century when the patriot Robert Emmet reputedly came here to plot rebellion.

WARM EMBRACE unites two customers *(below)* in Neary's Pub, an actors' meeting place in Dublin. Most Irish pubs serve both men and women, but a few remain staunchly all-male.

CONVIVIAL PUBS provide a setting for camaraderie, tall stories and recollections of incendiary politics

UNUSUAL CRONIES, a man and his dog frequent the elegant Victorian recesses of Dublin's Long Hall Pub. The barkeep is sweeping up, since 11:30 is the legal closing time in summer.

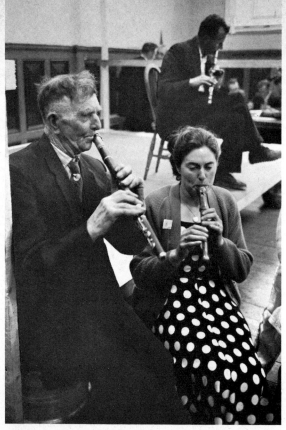

CULTURAL CONTEST in County Sligo draws performers from every part of Ireland. Harry Mullen, playing the flute in a duet with a recorder, is a competitor from nearby Galway.

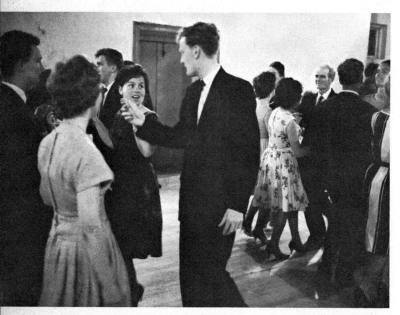

SUMMER FESTIVAL reunites young people of County Donegal home from their winter jobs in Scotland or Britain. They are moving through the intricate patterns of an Irish jig.

FRENETIC COUPLES twist in Strangford, County Down, as the stags observe impassively. The recent success of dance bands in Ireland reveals a growing tolerance towards frivolity.

Testimony to ancient struggles, the prehistoric fort of Dún Aonghus guards the Aran Islands. The stone fragments were placed to make

access to the inner walls (background) dangerous for invaders.

3

The Bitter Years

THE Irish did not acquire the habit of writing down their legends until they were encouraged to do so by the first Christian missionaries 400 years after the Crucifixion, but then, as now, they were a story-loving people, well fed for generations on glorious tales of their country's past. Not long after the missionaries' arrival, they produced a literature of folklore describing in vivid detail the Ireland of earlier centuries.

So it is that although factual Irish history does not begin until the Christian era, we have an imaginative, highly colored picture of Ireland in its pagan infancy, showing ancient kings who were surrounded by lawmakers, soldiers, musicians and poets and who presided over legislative and cultural assemblies. They were great days; the legendary kingdoms of Ireland were politically and militarily strong, and the land was soon to become a center of learning and the arts. It was Ireland's tragedy that the days of glory were not to endure; the triumphal years were to be followed by protracted centuries of degradation, persecution and exploitation.

At the time of Christ, Ireland was divided into provincial kingdoms with the same names that those areas bear today—Ulster, Munster, Leinster and Connaught, with the additional royal state of Meath, later taken into Leinster.

The early rulers were Gaelic Celts, with blond and reddish hair, who came to Ireland around 350 B.C. carrying iron weapons that enabled them to subdue the earlier inhabitants, a people from northern Spain who were armed with bronze. One of the most famous kings was Cormac MacArt of the line of Conn, who fortified and enlarged the ancient castle on the sacred hill of Tara, near what is now Dublin, and was supported by a renowned force of warriors called the Fianna, under the command of the legendary hero, Finn MacCool.

To qualify for membership in the Fianna, a recruit had to memorize 12 books of poetry and run through a thick forest, leaping over branches as high as his forehead and stooping under limbs as low as his knees without snapping a twig or tearing off a leaf. He also had to be able to pull a thorn out of his foot without breaking his stride.

THE next famous king after Cormac MacArt in Irish legend was Niall of the Nine Hostages, who ruled at Tara from 380 to 405 A.D., and whose descendants, the O'Neills, were lords of Ulster until 1603. Niall made a series of attacks on Britain and Normandy, then under declining Roman colonial government, and threatened for a while to conquer Wales and Scotland.

It is said that on one of these Irish raids against Britain, Niall's invaders brought back with them to Ulster a young prisoner named Patrick, a Latin-speaking Roman subject whose family was Christian. After several years as a sheep-herding slave in Ireland, Patrick escaped to the Continent, where he studied for the priesthood. In 432 he came back to Ireland as a bishop, charged with converting that nation to Christianity, a task that he carried out with spectacular success.

The acceptance of Saint Patrick's faith by the turbulent and mystic-minded Gaels changed the whole character of Ireland. The island became in the dark ages Western Europe's center of ecclesiastical learning, a land of monasteries that attracted students from all over the Continent and sent out missionaries, theological teachers and scholars to France, Germany, Austria and Switzerland, and even as far as Russia. Irish monks were in demand everywhere as Latin scribes whose skilled penmanship could preserve classical works of literature. At home, the monks produced the beautifully illuminated Latin scripts of the world-famous books of Kells and Durrow and wrote Celtic poems, romances, epics and histories in Gaelic, making Ireland the first European land north of Italy to produce a literature in its native language.

YET while Ireland flourished as a center of monastic culture engrossed in art and literature, it declined in political and military power. After Niall's death, there was no strong ruler or central government; the *Ard Ri*, or High King, at Tara was merely the chairman of a council of independent provincial kings who often defied him. In the Ninth and 10th Centuries, the island was easily overrun by savage seafaring Danish and Norwegian marauders, whose fleets were terrorizing England and Normandy at the same time.

The Scandinavians came first as pirate raiders, rowing up the Shannon and other rivers in their shallow-draft longboats, plundering monastic settlements while the frightened monks cowered above reach in the high Irish round towers. Then the Norsemen began to stay, building and fortifying the first towns in Ireland—Dublin, Cork, Limerick, Wexford and Waterford—and marrying Irish women. Such names as Loughlan and Doyle indicate Scandinavian origin. By the middle of the 10th Century the Norsemen held great areas of Ireland.

The Norse dominance was finally broken by King Brian Boru, the Irish counterpart of

Alfred the Great of England. In a series of bold military challenges, Brian drove the Danes out of Munster and captured their Dublin stronghold. Overcoming other Irish contenders to the throne he became in 1002 the first—and the last—undisputed native Christian King of all Ireland. Brian spent the next 10 years constructing fortresses and highways, and rebuilding churches and monasteries destroyed by the Scandinavians.

But Brian had made the mistake of marrying the beautiful but treacherous Gormflath, mother of Sitric, the half-Danish ruler of Dublin. Gormflath talked Brian into letting Sitric retain command of Dublin and plotted with her son and her brother, Maelmora, the provincial King of Leinster, to stage an uprising against Brian. She made a deal with Sigurd the Stout, Danish leader on the Orkney Islands, offering to marry him if he would send troops to Sitric's support. After some thought, Sigurd agreed to the proposition.

Brian was by then an old man of 74, but he marched his army from the royal camp at Kincora on the Shannon and met the combined Dublin-Leinster-Orkney force near Clontarf on the outskirts of Dublin on Good Friday, 1014. The fighting began at sunrise and lasted until sunset, a wild and bloody hand-to-hand struggle in which 20,000 men, the Irish in light linen tunics and the Danes in chain mail, slashed at each other with heavy swords and axes.

DESPITE his age, Brian had wanted to take command on the field, but his eldest son persuaded him to wait out the battle in a nearby tent. In the evening, when the beaten Danes began to flee, leaving 7,000 dead behind them, one of their leaders rushed past Brian's bodyguard and killed the King in his own tent.

The costly victory kept Ireland in the hands of the Irish—but only until the arrival of the Normans 150 years later.

These hardened conquerors, who had added England to their French possessions in 1066, were brought to Ireland by a disgruntled King of Leinster, Dermot MacMurrough, who sought their help in his fight for national power. But the Normans probably would have come anyway, sooner or later. Almost 20 years earlier, the Norman King of England, Henry II, had formally requested—and been granted—the Pope's permission to move into "irreligious" Ireland. Hungry for new baronial estates, Henry and his swashbuckling earls and knights had been eying Ireland for some time.

THE main Norman expeditionary force invited by Dermot landed near Waterford in 1170 under the command of the Earl of Pembroke, known as Strongbow. Although they spoke the French of Normandy, Pembroke and his companions had grown up in Wales, where the original Norman invaders of England had been given a free rein.

Most of these Norman Welsh felt little loyalty for the British king. After they had taken Waterford and Dublin, they urged Pembroke to break away from Britain and establish an independent Norman monarchy in Ireland.

But Pembroke was too hesitant and too wary of the hot-tempered Henry Plantagenet to try such a move. The King himself came to Ireland in the following year with an army of 4,000 men and 500 knights to stake his claim on the island and make it a part of his kingdom. Ignoring Rory O'Conor, reigning as Ireland's High King, Henry divided the land between the Normans and a few native provincial kings who agreed to pay annual tributes to Britain.

Henry also won over the Irish Catholic hierarchy; a synod at Cashel in 1171 abolished Gaelic liturgies and decreed that divine offices "shall be celebrated according to the usage of the Church of England."

Thus the pattern was set. British rule was to be enforced on Ireland for the next seven centuries. As in England and Wales, however, the Norman conquerors had to fight for the lands assigned to them by the Crown. Their grim castle fortresses sprang up all over the countryside. Outside their walls local wars flared between the mounted soldiers of the earls in suits of mail and conical iron helmets, and the clansmen of native chiefs. But eventually the Normans became, as the saying goes, more Irish than the Irish themselves; the Burkes, Joyces, Fitzgeralds, Roches and Barrys were all originally Norman families. But that merger was a long time in the making. For centuries, there was little but hatred between British and Irish.

When the first Parliament of Ireland was formed late in the 13th Century, only English colonists were allowed in it. Native Irish were excluded and parliamentary discussions were carried on in English and Norman French instead of Gaelic, the national language of Ireland at that time.

THE British stirred up more resentment in 1366 by enacting the Statutes of Kilkenny, which were intended to keep Anglo-Normans in Ireland from adopting "the manners, fashion and language of the Irish enemies." These laws, in effect for more than two centuries, made it illegal for the English to intermarry with the Irish, and even to admit Irish musicians and storytellers to their households. Any English subject heard speaking the Irish language was liable to have his land confiscated.

The hatred between the British and the Irish erupted into a fanatical holy war after the Protestant Reformation when Henry VIII and his Protestant successors tried to impose the practices of the new Church of England on Roman Catholic Ireland.

One of the first of Ireland's bloody religious uprisings broke out against Henry's daughter, Elizabeth I, in Munster in 1579. The Irish leader, Sir James Fitzmaurice, was killed, and a force of some 700 Spanish and Italian soldiers, sent by the Catholic Philip II of Spain and Pope Gregory XIII, was ruthlessly massacred near Dingle by the Queen's colonial troops, headed by Lord Grey and Sir Walter Raleigh. In reprisal for the rebellion, Elizabeth confiscated 200,000 acres of Catholic-owned land in southwest Ireland and turned the land over to Englishmen—a practice that was to become standard in the next two centuries. One tract was given to Raleigh, and it was here that he

planted the first Irish potato, destined to bring the country as much suffering and tragedy as it endured throughout the centuries of religious persecution.

Then came the last stand of Gaelic Catholic aristocracy against Elizabethan oppression. A nine-year war under two able Irish leaders, Hugh O'Neill, Earl of Tyrone, and Red Hugh O'Donnell, ended in famine and defeat. It was followed in 1607 by the sad "Flight of the Earls" into foreign exile. The departure of O'Neill, the last titled descendant of Niall, with some 98 other Northern Irish Catholic leaders, opened the way for Britain to establish the Ulster Plantation—a settlement of Scottish Presbyterians and English Protestants in colonies in the counties of the North. This northeast corner of Ireland, still loyal to the Crown today, was the only part of the country where the British were successful in introducing Protestantism—and Irish Catholic historians are quick to point out that it was done by colonization rather than by conversion. "They had to import them," one Irishman says.

ANOTHER savage, exhausting Protestant-Catholic war erupted in 1641 and continued for more than a decade. In August 1649, Oliver Cromwell, the stern Puritan leader of the temporarily kingless British Government, landed at Dublin with an expertly trained army of 20,000 men. He was determined to extinguish the spirit of rebellion forever. Cromwell and his soldiers displayed a zealous cruelty. They killed almost the entire population of the east coast town of Drogheda—civilian men, women and children as well as the defending soldiery. "It has pleased God," Cromwell wrote, "to bless our endeavours at Drogheda . . . the enemy were about 3,000 strong in the town . . . I believe we put to the sword the whole number of the defendants. I wish that all honest hearts may give the glory of this to God alone, to whom indeed the praise of this mercy belongs."

Cromwell's punitive expedition terrified Ireland for almost three years. Some 30,000 Irish soldiers in the armies that surrendered to him

EARLY IRELAND

Churches founded by St. Patrick   Monasteries flourishing in the 6th century

Important events and objects of ancient Ireland are shown here, starting with the Celtic invaders who landed in the southwest around 350 B.C. The early kings ruled vast domains like Munster from hill forts (as at Temuir Emain); a notable war pitted Queen Medb of Connacht against the Ulster hero Cú Chulainn. By the Third Century A.D., the Connacht kings had expanded and moved to Tara, in Meath; associated with Tara is the legend of Diarmaid and Gráinne. A Tara ruler was Niall of the Nine Hostages, who invaded England around 400 A.D. A century later a northern King, Fergus MacErc, took lands in Scotland. After Saint Patrick introduced Christianity into Ireland, many wooden churches were constructed; the monastic idea, as brought by Saints Enda and Finnian and disseminated by Saint Columba and others, resulted in monasteries which became centers of learning. Ireland's early culture culminated in the artistic objects labeled on the map.

Iona

St. Columba

Fergus MacErc

SCOTLAND

Cardonagh Stone Cross

Moville

Derry

Antiphonary of Bangor

Raphoe

Catach of St. Columba

ULSTER

Antrim

Bangor

Candida Casa

Cú Chulainn

Lough Erne Reliquiary

Emain Macha

Nendrum

St. Enda

Killala

Medb, Queen of Connacht

Armagh

Downpatrick

Isle of Man

Aghagower

Cruachain

Elphin

Athlone Plaque

Book of Kells

Monasterboice High Cross

Tara Brooch

IRISH SEA

Tuam

MEATH

Clonard

Tara

Clonmacnois High Cross Clonfert

Killossy

Aran

Diarmaid & Gráinne

Kildare

Glendalough Round Tower

CONNACHT

Dinn Rig

Niall of the Nine Hostages

Cashel Round Tower

LEINSTER

Ardagh Chalice

Aghade

Celtic Invaders

Temuir Emain

Cashel

Ahenny Stone Cross

Ossory

Ferns

St. David's

MUNSTER

Lismore

St. Finnian

WALES

Muskerry

ATLANTIC OCEAN

were allowed to go into exile in France and Spain, but several thousand civilians, including women and girls, were shipped as slaves to the West Indies and Virginia. It was estimated that these deportations and the 11 years of fighting and pillaging reduced the population of Ireland from 1,466,000 to 616,000.

BUT one of Cromwell's most incredibly inhuman punishments was yet to come in the terms of his peace settlement: almost every Irish landowner and landholding tenant east and south of the Shannon River was forced by law to give up his property and move to the less fertile, rocky and mountainous province of Connaught, or to County Clare on the west side of the river. When Cromwell was finished, Irish Catholics retained only one fourth of all the land in Ireland.

In 1685 the exhausted Irish felt a new and exciting surge of hope. A Catholic King, James II, came to the British throne, and he placed an Irish Catholic, Richard Talbot, the Earl of Tyrconnell, in command of the army in Ireland, which became staffed with Catholic officers. The law against allowing Catholics to hold legal and civic offices was suspended, and judges of the Roman faith began to preside over the courts.

But just as the Crown began to restore land to Catholic owners, James Stuart broke with his Tory supporters in London and was replaced by a Protestant King, William III, the Prince of Orange. James fled to France and then to Ireland, seeking the support of Tyrconnell's Catholic army. William followed with an army of 36,000 for the showdown with James at the Battle of the Boyne in 1690. Naturally the English Protestant and Scottish Presbyterian colonists of the Ulster Plantation came to his aid.

Just as naturally the Catholic Irish backed James, and when he retreated in defeat from the Boyne, the hope for a peaceful Catholic Ireland went with him. When the war dragged to an end at Limerick a year later, there was another great exodus of Irish soldiers to the Continent. This was celebrated in Irish songs and poetry as "The Flight of the Wild Geese."

Now Ireland seemed to be crushed into complete submission, with its leaders gone and its people facing a long and dark century of suppression under the Penal Laws, enacted in vengeance for the Catholic opposition to William. These laws, which were not entirely repealed until 1829, aimed to make the Irish Catholics "insignificant slaves, fit for nothing but to hew wood and draw water." The British statesman Edmund Burke described their provisions as "a machine . . . as well fitted for the oppression, impoverishment and degradation of a people, and the debasement in them of human nature itself, as ever proceeded from the perverted ingenuity of man."

THE earlier Kilkenny statutes had not been based on religious discrimination. In medieval Ireland both the British colonists and the natives had been Catholics. The Penal Laws assumed, on the other hand, that every Catholic was an enemy outlaw, regardless of wealth or rank or English lineage, and reduced virtually all Irish of the Roman faith—the great majority of the population—to poverty with no rights of citizenship.

Catholics were forbidden to vote or to hold office and were barred from military and civil service, the legal profession and teaching. No Catholic schools were permitted and children were allowed to attend only Protestant schools. A Catholic was not even entitled to own a horse valued at more than five pounds; if a good horse, worth more, were found in his possession, a Protestant could take it from him and force him to accept five pounds as legal payment. Religious rights were severely restricted. Only those few priests who were willing to forswear allegiance to James and the Stuart line were permitted to conduct services. Masses were said secretly in the fields and private homes, with a few men standing guard to watch for British patrols.

Estates owned by Catholics were broken up and confiscated as further penalties for the support given to James II. One of the Penal Laws prohibited a Catholic from leaving all of his land to one son; it had to be divided equally among all of his sons. This meant that a small farm often was broken into five or six tiny tracts, useless for supporting a family.

And so dawned the glorious Georgian 18th Century in Ireland, with a handful of newly rich Protestant landowners in the so-called Anglo-Irish ascendancy building gorgeous castles in the country and mansions in Dublin. Meanwhile the Catholic majority, thousands of farming families, lived in near-starvation on potatoes. Jonathan Swift, the dean of Dublin's Anglican Saint Patrick's Cathedral, became so enraged by the plight of the Irish people that he urged them to burn everything from Britain except its coal, and wrote "A Modest Proposal," a savage essay suggesting that Irish children could be fattened up and served on English tables. An anonymous street song came to be sung as Ireland's national anthem:

> Oh, Paddy dear, and did ye hear the news
>   that's goin' round?
> The shamrock is by law forbid to grow
>   on Irish ground.
> No more Saint Patrick's Day we'll keep,
>   his color can't be seen,
> For there's a cruel law ag'in the Wearin'
>   o' the Green . . .

Treated as criminal outlaws, the Irish Catholics began to resort to criminal acts of revenge, organizing secret armed bands with such names as the White Boys and the Cork Boys. They prowled the country at night, lynching Protestant land agents and new tenants who had replaced evicted Catholic farmers, burning stables and tearing down fences. Armed groups called houghers hamstrung or massacred sheep and cattle to warn against continued evictions; other bands of men raped, kidnaped and held girls and women for ransom.

One section of the Penal Laws backfired on the British. Ruinous restrictions on Irish industry and tithes for the support of the Anglican Church sorely chafed the Scotch-Irish Presbyterian manufacturers of Ulster. The earliest wholesale emigrations of Irish to America in the 18th Century were from the North. The Scotch-Irish, seeking political freedom from Britain, played a major role in the American Revolution. Among them was General Andrew Jackson, whose parents were born in County Antrim. Four signers of the Declaration of Independence were born in Ireland and five others were of Irish descent.

News of the American revolt and the French Revolution in 1789 stirred up a strong spirit of agitation in Ulster. When Theobald Wolfe Tone, a young Protestant lawyer, formed the Society of United Irishmen in 1791 ("to abolish all unnatural religious distinctions, to unite all Irishmen against the unjust influence of Great Britain . . ."), that movement's first headquarters was in Belfast. Alarmed by this rumbling, the Government passed a Catholic relief act in 1793, allowing those Catholics who owned land worth 40 shillings or more to hold some voting rights and minor civil service jobs and to have education privileges. They were still barred, however, from membership in the Irish Parliament.

That same year, France went to war with Britain. Tone, with the backing of an estimated 150,000 United Irishmen, persuaded the French to support him in a war of insurrection. Wearing the uniform of a French general, he sailed from Brest to Bantry Bay in 1796 with a French fleet carrying a force of 15,000 soldiers. But the admirals in command of the warships were easily discouraged by stormy weather and turned back from the Irish coast without landing.

THE United Irishmen staged a disorganized uprising by themselves in 1798 which was put down by troops under the command of the same Lord Cornwallis who had surrendered earlier to George Washington at the battle of Yorktown. Tone came again, too late, with another French contingent; this time he was captured. Instead of being executed before a firing squad, as he requested, he was sentenced to be hanged like a common criminal, and so he committed suicide in a British prison cell.

Tone was followed in 1803 by the gallant Robert Emmet, too dreamily idealistic to be a successful revolutionist; his planned outbreak ended in failure. As the historian Edmund Curtis notes in *A History of Ireland*, however, the execution of Emmet and his memorable courtroom speech had a greater impact on the Irish than any act of Parliament or political event. Emmet cried from the dock: "When my country takes her place among the nations of the earth, then, and not till then, let my epitaph be written." Every Irish revolt from then on was launched with the fervent hope that it would write Emmet's epitaph.

EVEN before the uprising of 1798, William Pitt, the British Prime Minister, had decided that the only way Ireland could be kept under British control would be to enact an Act of Union, transferring legislative control of the country from Dublin to the British Parliament at Westminster, and merging the Irish economy into that of Britain. Ireland, in other words, was to cease its existence as a national entity and was to become, like Wales and Scotland, a part of the United Kingdom.

The Act of Union was fought vigorously in the Irish Parliament, not only by such patriots as Henry Grattan but by the Protestants of the Anglo-Irish ascendancy, who controlled the economy and who were not anxious to pay British taxes. Grattan's last plea is highly esteemed by the oratory-loving Irish: "Yet I do not give up my country," he said. "I see her in a swoon but she is not dead; though in her tomb she lies helpless and motionless, still on her lips is the spirit of life and on her cheeks the glow of beauty."

But Pitt passed the act in 1800, buying votes with £1,260,000 in cash and with 48 new or promoted titles in the Irish peerage—one of the most shameful political bribery transactions in history. One of the promises that he made to obtain passage was that Catholics would be included among the Irish representatives seated in the British houses of Parliament.

Pitt did put this proposal before George III, but the obstinate King turned it down. The Penal Law against representation for the millions of Irish Catholics was not repealed until 1829, when Daniel O'Connell won his hard fight for his people's legislative emancipation.

The most colorful personality in modern Irish history, O'Connell was a charming and gifted Kerryman who gave up a brilliant career as a trial lawyer to serve as a champion of the Irish peasants. He had a special talent for arousing great mass meetings of tens of thousands with dazzling oratory. His powerful voice could be heard at the outside edges of the huge crowds. He climaxed his battle for emancipation by winning an election to the House of Commons at Clare in 1828 in defiance of the Penal Laws.

As a Catholic, O'Connell could not take his Parliamentary seat, of course, but his show of strength forced the British Government to grant almost complete recognition of Catholic rights a year later. When he joined the House, O'Connell supported the Whigs against the Tories in return for favors to Ireland. His critics claimed that he was often taken in by the Whig Government, which did nothing to relieve the oppression of O'Connell's peasant supporters by absentee British landlords. The Emancipation Act, in fact, deprived small Irish farmers of the right to vote; only the larger Catholic property holders retained the franchise.

WHEN the Whigs went out of office in 1841, O'Connell was already campaigning for repeal of the Act of Union. He insisted on trying to win this difficult objective by peaceful means; he abhorred any display of violence that might cause bloodshed. After rallying all of Ireland to his support, he planned a giant mass demonstration for repeal of the Act of Union on the battlefield at Clontarf, where Brian Boru had defeated the Danes in 1014.

The day before the mass meeting, which thousands of Irish were ready to attend, the British Government ordered it canceled and threatened to break it up by armed force if the order was disobeyed. O'Connell called off the meeting. That ended his political career. His disappointed followers turned away from him, and he died a few years later, broken in health and spirit.

The defeat of O'Connell's unfulfilled effort to win repeal of the Act of Union was followed two years later, in 1845, by the worst calamity ever to hit Ireland—the famine caused by the potato blight, which destroyed for three years the crop that more than half of the people depended on for food.

THE disaster of the famine killed a million and a half Irish people and forced another million to emigrate from the country between 1846 and 1851. Such starvation arose because poverty-stricken masses of rural people, with no money to buy food, had been reduced to eating nothing except potatoes, which could be grown for a few pennies on a small plot of land. Even before the blight ruined the potatoes, the Irish peasants had been plagued by hunger in the summer months, when the previous year's crop was eaten and new plants had not yet produced food.

Land to grow potatoes on was scarce and difficult to rent; it was more profitable for a large landowner—usually a wealthy man who lived in England—to raise cattle for export than to grow crops.

The British Government did little to relieve the suffering caused by the blight. Beef, pork, lamb and grain raised in Ireland were sold for export, as usual. A small farmer with six children to feed still had to sell his wheat or oats in order to pay his rent while his family went hungry. Otherwise he would be evicted.

Turning Ireland's food products over to famine sufferers instead of letting them go to market, or stopping rents or evictions as an emergency relief measure, seemed inconceivable to the British officials of that time. As Cecil Woodham-Smith points out in her definitive study of the famine, *The Great Hunger*, the British believed religiously in the *laissez-faire* theory of economics; a government must never interfere with private commerce or with the rights of a landlord to make a profit and evict a tenant.

By the same token, the Government itself did not wish to compete with private trade by buying and distributing food. When Prime Minister Robert Peel took the drastic step of buying American corn for distribution in Ireland, he did so with the utmost secrecy. When the Government was finally faced with providing emergency soup kitchens and large-scale food-dispensing centers in Ireland, nobody except a few Army commissary officers knew how to handle the task.

Being unprepared ideologically or otherwise to cope with the problem, the British could provide little help for Ireland. The Irish could only feel that they were being left to starve to death; the British, it was charged, were using the famine to carry on the work of Cromwell.

IN the same mood of bitterness which prevailed long after the famine years, the Irish rallied behind a new leader, Charles Stewart Parnell, who carried on the banner of Home Rule that had slipped from Dan O'Connell's hands. Parnell was a Protestant landowner, but he rose to prominence and popularity in Ireland as a dedicated defender of small farmers suffering from landlord exploitation. He went on to greater fame and power as leader of the Irish faction in the House of Commons.

But in 1890, when Parnell was at the crest of his prestige and influence, he was named co-respondent in a divorce case brought by William O'Shea, one of his political followers, against his wife Kitty. Parnell never denied the charge, and after Mrs. O'Shea was divorced he married her. At another time in another country, such a scandal might have been overlooked, but in the Victorian era and in severely moral Ireland, it meant that Parnell's career was finished. The majority of Parnell's supporters deserted their fallen chief. The cause of Home Rule had been dealt a staggering blow. The Irish could hope only for better luck in the approaching 20th Century.

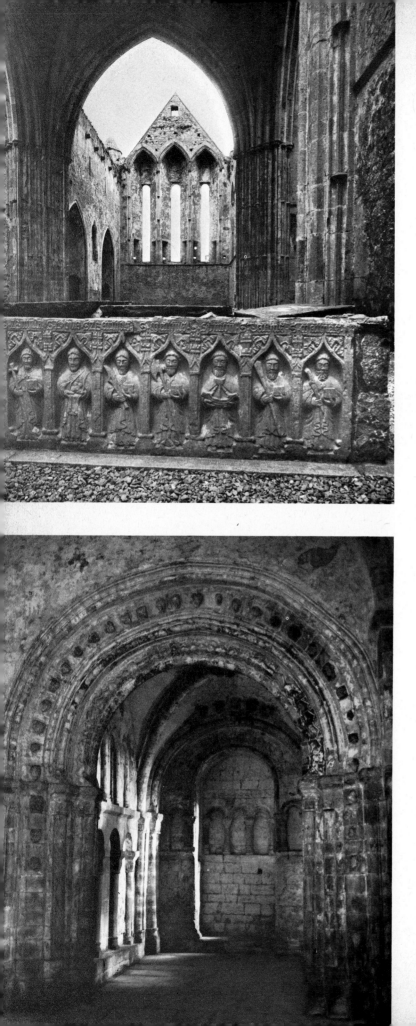

STONE SAINTS adorn a medieval tomb in the cathedral on the Rock of Cashel in Tipperary. The church is roofless because an 18th Century Protestant archbishop used the lead roof in building his palace.

Undying Echoes of a Heroic Past

Long before Europe's Middle Ages, Ireland was a center of artistic and intellectual excellence. Barely a century after Saint Patrick introduced the Christian faith, Irish missionaries were traveling to Britain and the Continent. If the Sixth Century was a time of flourishing monasteries, the Seventh opened the Golden Age of Art. With new motifs from Europe and new techniques, Irish craftsmen achieved a peak of sophisticated ornamentation in metalwork and manuscripts. This resplendent period was interrupted by the raids of barbarous Scandinavians in the late Eighth Century. During the era of England's domination, the memory of Ireland's religious, political and cultural freedom comforted the soul of an oppressed people.

SUPERB SANCTUARY, the small Cormac's Chapel at Cashel is decorated by a Romanesque doorway. The most remarkable building of the 12th Century, it has a wealth of carving and ornamentation.

IMPOSING STRUCTURES top the Rock of Cashel *(opposite)*, which was until 1101 a seat of Munster kings. The cathedral *(right)*, Saint Patrick's Cross *(left)* and the Round Tower *(center)* dominate the hill.

*MEDIEVAL GLORY lingers
in a multitude of remarkable
religious objects created
with unique Irish design*

THE CROSS OF CONG originally enshrined what was reputed to be a sliver of the True Cross. Plated in copper, the 12th Century crucifix measures two and a half feet tall.

THE BOOK OF KELLS, a Ninth Century illuminated gospel *(opposite),* is Ireland's most famous antiquity. On this page, the topmost line is the Latin word "Nativitas."

THE ARDAGH CHALICE is seven inches high *(below),* but so heavy two hands are required to lift it. Celtic decoration makes it the masterpiece of the Eighth Century.

REFUGE FROM ATTACKS was provided Ireland's medieval scholars by round towers like the one near the ruined monastery at Glendalough, County Wicklow. Built around 1100 A.D., the tower served mainly as a belfry. But when Vikings invaded, the Irish monks crowded into the tower and pulled their ladders up into the only doorway, which was 10 feet above the ground.

THE MASSACRE OF DROGHEDA, a County Louth city, was staged in 1649 by Oliver Cromwell, shown at left above mounted on his white charger. Seeking to avenge English deaths in Ulster, Cromwell slaughtered 3,500 people, both soldiers and townsfolk, opening a period of oppression lasting for 30 years.

BATTLE OF THE BOYNE, won by William III of Orange in 1690 *(below),* dashed Irish hopes for Roman Catholic rule. Just as the Catholic King of England James II was restoring rights to the Irish, the Protestant William *(center)* replaced him, defeated him at Boyne, and crushed the Irish rebels.

FAMINE killed more than a million
people in the late 1840s when
a fungus blight attacked
the potato crop and destroyed it

SEVERE STARVATION caused so many deaths that corpses were piled on carts *(above)* and buried without coffins. Although some food and money came from English and Irish charities, poor communications prevented effective distribution of relief.

DEVASTATING BLIGHT in 1845 destroyed the food which more than half the Irish ate exclusively, the potato. Peasants like this mother and son spaded stubble fields looking for un-diseased plants. The fungus attacked again in 1846 and 1848.

MASS PROTEST against the shortage of rations brought starving families to storm government workhouses, which sheltered the needy. With the workhouses full, the government instituted a relief program but in the crisis the system collapsed.

FORCED EVICTION drove tenants from their homes *(below)*. In order to keep the evicted from returning, landlords had the local sheriff *(on horseback)* raze, or "tumble," the cottages. The cleared area was subsequently changed into pasture land.

MASS EMIGRATION from Ireland to America occurred during the famine years. From 1847 to 1855 more than one million emigrants bade farewell to their relatives remaining behind and boarded decrepit cargo ships bound for the United States.

Soldiers survey the gutted interior of Dublin's General Post Office, virtually demolished by British shell fire during the unsuccessful

1916 Easter Week rising which led to the Anglo-Irish war.

4

The Troubles

THE Irish are quick to admit their notoriety for fighting among themselves. A woman in Athlone was talking recently with an American about the unanimously warm welcome given to President Kennedy when he visited her country in 1963. "It was the first time everybody in Ireland agreed on anything since the British tried to put through conscription in 1918," she said.

That earlier agreement among the contrary Irish minds in the closing months of World War I was an ominous one. Centuries of oppression and cruelty had haunted Ireland; now the nation was to experience an outburst of violence rivaling any of the savagery of the past. The country was well aware at the war's end that thousands of volunteers had already given service with the British Army in France. It was seething with indignation over the execution of 15 leaders of the 1916 Easter Week rebellion in Dublin. In a gesture of defiance toward the British, the surviving senior officer of that brief uprising, Eamon de Valera, had just been elected in County Clare to Daniel O'Connell's old seat in the British Parliament. John Dillon, head of the Irish delegation in the House of Commons, warned the British Prime Minister, David Lloyd George, that forcing compulsory military service on the Irish might be the last straw.

Lloyd George nevertheless pushed the Irish Conscription Bill through Parliament. In outrage, all of Ireland's divided political factions rose together against Britain. A few months after the armistice, when de Valera's Sinn Fein movement declared Ireland's independence and started an armed revolt, the whole country, except for four pro-British counties in Ulster, was united behind it.

THE earlier Easter Week rebellion of 1916, which began the series of events that culminated in the winning of Irish independence, had had no such popular support at its inception. Since the fall of Parnell in 1890, the Irish Home Rule movement had broken into several conservative and radical groups. Eventually there were at least 15 active revolutionary groups. None of them possessed a large following; all were divided within their own ranks.

The extreme nationalist faction, for example, was made up of an alliance between the Sinn Fein (Ourselves Alone) Party, under the leadership of Arthur Griffith, and the Irish Republican Brotherhood, headed by Tom Clarke, who had spent 15 years as a political prisoner in an English jail. Clarke wanted an independent Irish republic, as did most of the Sinn Feiners. Griffith favored a monarchy, with the English monarch holding two separate roles—King of England and King of Ireland—and separate British and Irish parliamentary governments.

The nationalist factions had come close to starting an armed war against the violently anti-Home Rule and anti-Catholic unionists of Ulster shortly before the outbreak of World War I. The Ulster Irish, led by Edward Carson, were Presbyterians and Anglicans. They were violently opposed to Home Rule because they refused to be governed by Catholics in Dublin.

When the British Government offered Ireland a mild form of Home Rule in 1910 ("full self-government in regard to purely Irish affairs"), Carson threatened to set up a separate Ulster government by armed force. He openly ran guns into the North and in 1912 organized the Ulster Volunteers, a military auxiliary. Carson was backed by the generals of the British Army's occupation troops in Ireland, who warned the Government that they would not suppress a revolt in Ulster.

THE Irish nationalists hastened to form their own military organizations, too, smuggling guns into the country and drilling troops in preparation for a fight against Carson. The Irish Republican Brotherhood and a few Sinn Feiners organized the soldiers of the Irish Volunteers. One of the first recruits to sign up was Eamon de Valera, a serious young teacher of mathematics. The Labour Party in Dublin established the Irish Citizen Army, hailed by Lenin as the first Communist army in Europe. It was commanded by the fiery James Connolly and its secretary was Sean O'Casey, not yet a famous dramatist.

When Britain went to war against Germany in 1914, many of the Irish Volunteers, the military arm of Sinn Fein, enlisted in the British Army. Carson's Ulster Volunteers joined the British Army as a unit. A grateful Parliament promised to do nothing about Home Rule until the war ended. Now free from the threat of attack from the North, the Irish rebels began to make other plans for their Volunteer and Citizen Army soldiers, who were drilling and marching in public with rifles on their shoulders. One day, under the eyes of British officers, the Volunteer troops even staged a sham attack on the Dublin Post Office.

The citizen-soldiers claimed that they served "neither King George nor the Kaiser, but Ireland." Yet all of them believed in the old slogan of Gaelic insurrectionaries, "England's misfortune is Ireland's opportunity." Irish sympathizers in New York and Sir Roger Casement, an Irish agent in Germany, sought arms and ammunition from the Germans. The Volunteers and the Citizen Army joined forces and plotted the capture of Dublin. The date set was Monday of Easter Week, 1916, when most of the officers in the British military garrisons would be out of town attending the races at Fairyhouse.

The rebellion was doomed before its start by hasty and poorly coordinated planning and the inadequate strength of the Irish forces. Eoin MacNeill, chief of the Volunteers, was opposed to staging an armed revolt while England was at war, and the other leaders did not let him know of their plans until the last minute. Furious, he ordered the attack called off.

The plotters decided to go on with the uprising. Most of their followers did not hear until too late that MacNeill's order had been countermanded. In several provincial cities where attacks were to be launched at the same time as the assault on Dublin, nothing happened. The men reporting for action on Monday morning in Dublin numbered only around 1,200 instead of the 2,400 that were expected.

Through another mix-up in messages the *Aud*, a German ship carrying arms for the uprising, reached Tralee Bay in Kerry three days before her scheduled arrival. Trying to head her off, Sir Roger Casement raced to Tralee by submarine but arrived too late. The *Aud* was surrounded by the British and blown up by its crew. After rowing ashore in a small boat, Casement was arrested by local police and was later hanged in London for treason.

DESPITE these confusions, the small contingent of rebels captured several key points in Dublin on Monday, and established a provisional Irish Republic Government headquarters at the Post Office, hoisting a green, white and orange Irish flag on the roof of the building. Patrick Pearse, commander of this new Irish Republican Army, read on the Post Office steps the now-famous proclamation that begins: "Irishmen and Irishwomen: In the name of God and of the dead generations from which she receives her old tradition of nationhood,

MAJOR GROUPS IN THE REVOLUTION

SINN FEIN: Organized as a political party in 1904, Sinn Fein (Ourselves Alone) demanded the political and cultural independence of all of Ireland.

IRISH REPUBLICAN BROTHERHOOD: An offshoot of Sinn Fein, the I.R.B. wanted independence for Ireland, but favored continued alliance with Britain.

IRISH VOLUNTEERS: A military group organized by members of the I.R.B. and Sinn Fein, it began the Easter Week uprising of 1916.

IRISH REPUBLICAN ARMY: The Irish Volunteers became the I.R.A. when the independence of Ireland was proclaimed during the Easter Week uprising.

ULSTER VOLUNTEERS: Organized by Ulster Irishmen who opposed independence, this military group enlisted in the British Army in World War I.

IRISH CITIZEN ARMY: This group was the military auxiliary of the Irish Labour Party, which demanded immediate and total independence.

FIANNA FAIL: A political party, Fianna Fail (Warriors of Destiny) was opposed to the partition of Ulster from Southern Ireland.

BRITISH FORCES: Troops attempting to put down the rebellion of 1918-1921 were divided into three groups: the Royal Irish Constabulary; the elite Auxiliaries, an organization of former British officers who had served in World War I; and the Black and Tans, a force of former British enlisted men.

Ireland, through us, summons her children to her flag and strikes for her freedom."

The British, taken by surprise, rushed Army troops into the city and pinned down the rebels under heavy machine gun and artillery fire. A gunboat on the River Liffey demolished most of the buildings on O'Connell Street, and the Post Office was burned. After holding out all week, the Irish were finally forced to surrender on Saturday.

In the fighting, 56 Republican soldiers and 216 Dublin civilians were killed or died from wounds. The British reported 130 dead.

This opening battle of the revolution stirred many Irish deeply, but most of Ireland viewed the destruction and bloodshed with glum indifference or irritation, regarding the whole performance as a reckless and unnecessary outburst by a few hotheaded political fanatics. Easter Week sparked no patriotic feeling in the many Irish families who had sons fighting with British forces in the trenches in France.

Then the British authorities began to put the leaders of the rebellion to death, sending three or four of them at a time before firing squads after quick and secret court martial trials. James Connolly, badly wounded at the Post Office, was carried to the execution yard on a stretcher and propped up before the firing squad in a chair.

The results were immediate. The Irish people stiffened in anger. Annoyed embarrassment was swept away by a fierce and choking flush of national pride. The Catholic bishop of Limerick, Edward Thomas O'Dwyer, denounced the British general, Sir John Maxwell, who had ordered the executions: "Personally I regard your action with horror and I believe that it has outraged the conscience of the country."

Pictures of the executed rebels were hung on cottage walls beside those of Robert Emmet and the Sacred Heart of Jesus. The spirit of revolution that the Easter Week men had failed to inspire in their march on Dublin had been aroused by their deaths in the prison yard. The stage was set for the next and final fight for freedom in 1918.

LEADERSHIP in the Sinn Fein movement was now more or less thrust upon de Valera; all the other chiefs except Arthur Griffith were dead, and Griffith, never a militant Republican, had not fought in Easter Week. De Valera had distinguished himself in that action, commanding a small Volunteer detachment. He had been sentenced to death with the other leaders but his sentence had been suspended and he was imprisoned in England.

There he found himself heading the surviving die-hard Republicans. After Easter Week, known and suspected rebels from all over Ireland were rounded up and shipped with the surrendered Dublin insurgents to jails and internment camps in Britain, where they turned to de Valera for guidance. A distant and stern man, with no warm small talk, he was nevertheless trusted and deeply respected. One of his fellow prisoners at Dartmoor and Lewes

recalls: "He became the leader of us all without any consultation, debate or election. Whenever any proposal was made or discussed, the first question everyone asked was: 'What does Dev think of it?' "

The political prisoners, numbering more than 2,500, were too much for the British jailers to handle. They were released, some late in 1916 and the rest in 1917, and welcomed in Ireland with wildly enthusiastic torchlight parades.

WHEN de Valera was let out of the gates of Pentonville jail in England, he was handed a telegram telling him that he had been nominated as the Sinn Fein candidate in an East Clare by-election for a vacant seat in the House of Commons. No one could serve in Commons without taking an oath of allegiance to the King, which the Sinn Feiners refused to do. But that did not stop them from entering election contests to show their popular support and to discredit the rival Irish Parliamentary Party, which favored moderate Home Rule with continued membership in the British Empire.

Sinn Fein had now become an out-and-out movement for the establishment of an Irish republic. De Valera's candidacy in East Clare was watched by all of Ireland and Britain as a crucial test of Sinn Fein strength.

De Valera opened his campaign by reading the Republican manifesto that Pearse had spoken on the Post Office steps in Dublin. That, he said, was what he stood for. His Parliamentary Party opponent pleaded against having Irishmen "shot down in a futile and insane attempt to establish an Irish Republic." De Valera won the election by a 2 to 1 majority.

The line was now clearly drawn, but the British were in no mood to give up Ireland while they were fighting a war. Eighty-four Republicans were arrested in the following month.

Officially installed as the Sinn Fein leader, with the support of Arthur Griffith, the party's founder, de Valera denied pro-German sympathy and discouraged armed violence against the British for the duration of the war. In 1918, when Prime Minister Lloyd George aroused bitterness with his plan for conscription, most of the Sinn Feiners were eager for another Easter Week uprising. De Valera had difficulty persuading them to maintain what he called "passive resistance." They called a general strike instead, stopping all transportation and all work for one day of protest in every city except Belfast.

Robert Brennan, one of de Valera's aides, recalls that during the conscription uproar a young man pedaled his bicycle 45 miles one day from a town in County Offaly to the Sinn Fein headquarters in Dublin, carrying an empty burlap sack.

"We had a meeting last night," he said, "and we decided to meet the menace of conscription by passive resistance, so they sent me in to pick up a bag of bombs."

In April 1918, when Sinn Fein campaigns to prevent conscription were being organized, the police captured an Irish agent who had been landed from a German submarine on the Galway coast. The British Government charged that he had been arranging a conspiracy between the Germans and Sinn Fein, and immediately deported de Valera and 73 other Sinn Fein leaders, without trials, to prisons in England.

DE VALERA and most of these party chiefs were still in prison when the war ended. But the I.R.A. had one dedicated and highly skilled leader still at large, a husky, handsome man named Michael Collins. In January 1919, when the Sinn Fein convened the first meeting of Dail Eireann, the Irish rebel Parliament, and declared the independence of the Irish Republic, Collins was only 29 years old. He had, however, already spent two years organizing intelligence networks and combat units. Collins seemed fearless; while the British were offering £10,000 for his arrest, he rode his bicycle calmly through the Dublin streets with a revolver in his pocket.

For all his charm, Collins was a completely ruthless terrorist. His squad of gunmen in trench coats and slouch hats killed 14 secret agents of the British in Dublin on November 21, 1920, a day afterward known as Bloody Sunday. Most of the victims were shot in their beds or getting out of bed to answer a knock on the door. One agent's wife tried to shield her husband while he was climbing out a window. Collins' men dragged her away and fired seven shots into her husband, leaving him dead and hanging halfway out the window.

That afternoon the British soldiers and police surrounded Croke Park, where a big crowd was watching a Dublin-Tipperary football game. The official plan was to close the exits and search the crowd for hidden weapons, but a group of soldiers opened fire. One player and 11 spectators were killed and many others injured. Thirty revolvers were dropped on the ground by frantically running spectators.

EARLIER, in February 1919, Collins had designed a plan that enabled de Valera to escape from Lincoln jail, sending him a cake with a key to his cell door concealed inside it. But during the revolution of the next three years, which the Irish refer to with quiet understatement as The Troubles, it was Collins, rather than de Valera, who directed the Republican Army. As President of the resistance Government, de Valera was more concerned with policy than with fighting, and he spent a year and a half in the United States trying to win American support and money for his cause.

The Big Fellow, as Collins was called, fought an evasive hit-and-run war. He avoided pitched battles like that of Easter Week. The I.R.A. seldom numbered as many as 15,000 men, all untrained civilians, poorly armed and with few motor vehicles. They faced a combined British Army and constabulary of more than 70,000 mobile troops. Collins divided his men into tactical units, which he referred to as flying columns, each with 75 to 100 men, and often with fewer than that.

A flying column was usually assembled for a quick raid on a police barracks or for an ambush on a convoy of British troops on a lonely rural road. After the attack the force would disperse and scatter into the fields or bogs. The next morning some of the I.R.A. men would be working innocently at their jobs as farmers, teachers or storekeepers; others would go into hiding until the next assignment.

These small harassments wore down the British more effectively than might be imagined. They were carried out relentlessly and incessantly all over Ireland; the authorities could never be sure when or where the I.R.A. would strike next.

BEWILDERED by the invisible enemy, the British could do little more than impose early curfews, search homes in the hope of finding a suspect and carry out harsh acts of reprisal. Erskine Childers, an English convert to the Irish crusade, wrote in 1920 for a London newspaper this description of Dublin in the curfew hours: "As the citizens go to bed, the barracks spring to life. Lorries, tanks, and armoured searchlight cars muster in fleets. . . . Think of raiding a private house at dead of night in a tank. . . . A thunder of knocks; no time to dress (even for a woman alone) or the door will crash in. On opening, in charge the soldiers—literally charge—with fixed bayonets and in full war-kit. . . . Imagine the moral effect of such a procedure on the young officers and men told off for this duty! Is it any wonder that gross abuses occur: looting, wanton destruction, brutal severity to women?"

The British were reluctant to assign these Gestapo-type raids to Army units because the Government denied that a state of war existed in Ireland. The task of coping with the I.R.A. was left mainly to the police force of the Royal Irish Constabulary—enlarged for the emergency with two special temporary-duty groups, each with 15,000 tough World War I veterans recruited in England and Scotland through newspaper ads offering "rough and dangerous" military service in Ireland.

These two special groups, filled with irresponsible and hard-drinking youngsters just out of the trenches, were the Black and Tans and the Auxiliary Cadets, an elite corps consisting only of ex-officers. The Black and Tans,

so-called because of their makeshift uniforms of Irish Constabulary dark green and army khaki, were paid 10 shillings a day. Although they became notorious in the literature and motion pictures of The Troubles as brutal and reckless killers, they were actually less feared in Ireland than the better-dressed and supposedly higher-principled pound-a-day Auxiliaries.

The Black and Tans burned and looted such towns as Ennistymon, Lahinch and Trim, but it was the Auxiliaries who set fire to the entire business district of Cork in reprisal for an I.R.A. attack on an Auxiliary patrol earlier the same day. Reinforced by the Black and Tans, they held back with pointed guns the firemen who came to the burning buildings. The Auxiliaries were well equipped with trucks and armored cars and roamed all over the country, committing drunken vandalisms and terrifying old people and children.

The Auxiliary Cadets' commanding officer, General F. P. Crozier, resigned from his post in 1921 because he was unable to maintain discipline. Crozier gave up in disgust after discovering that an Auxiliary officer had ordered his men to capture the outspoken pro-Republican Catholic bishop of Killaloe, Dr. Michael Fogarty, and to drown him in a weighted sack in the River Shannon. Luckily for the bishop, he happened to be out of town on the day that the Auxiliaries came to pick him up.

SENSELESS and sadistic acts of cruelty were frequently practiced by the I.R.A. as well as by the Black and Tans and the Auxiliaries. In County Clare a party of rebels buried a British magistrate up to his neck in sand just below the high-tide mark on a seaside beach so that the rising water would slowly cover his face. The next day his tormentors found him still alive. They dug him up and replanted him closer to the incoming waves, again leaving him to watch the tide creep up to his neck and chin. This time the rising waters finished the job.

The single act of the revolution that aroused more worldwide interest and sympathy for Ireland's struggle than any military terrorism was the long hunger strike of Terence MacSwiney, the Lord Mayor of Cork, after he was imprisoned in England in the autumn of 1920.

A few months earlier, MacSwiney's predecessor, Lord Mayor Thomas MacCurtain, who was also the commander of the Cork Brigade of the I.R.A., had been shot in his home by British police. When MacSwiney replaced the murdered mayor he also assumed his I.R.A. duties. He was conducting an Army meeting in City Hall when he was arrested and charged with possessing documents "likely to cause disaffection to His Majesty."

MACSWINEY claimed that citizens of the Irish Republic could be tried only in Republican courts—which the Sinn Fein Government was then operating in 27 counties. In protest against the infringement of his and others' legal rights, he said, he would refuse food while in jail. Ten other I.R.A. men arrested with him also began a hunger strike. After 70 days of fasting, MacSwiney was still alive, and many British and American people who had paid little attention to the revolution in Ireland up to that time were following the daily reports on his condition with growing compassion. MacSwiney died on October 24, 1920, his 74th day on the hunger strike. Two other prisoners died at the same time.

An honor guard of uniformed I.R.A. soldiers and a procession of thousands of Irish marched behind MacSwiney's Irish flag-draped coffin when it was taken through the streets of London before being shipped to Cork. Not a sound of protest was heard from the crowds of respectfully silent British spectators.

In 1921, the third year of the revolt, the Republican Army and the Irish people were still far from subdued and the British authorities were preparing to launch what Winston Churchill called "the most unlimited exercise of rough-handed force."

But before the British could undertake drastic measures, King George V intervened with a public plea for a peaceful settlement. A few days later de Valera received an invitation to confer with Prime Minister Lloyd George. A truce was called.

The big stumbling block in the peace-treaty talks that followed was the question of the six northeastern Ulster counties, which had shortly before been partitioned from the rest of Ireland as a province of the United Kingdom with its own parliamentary government. De Valera was willing to compromise on his earlier demand for an Irish republic and accept membership in the British Commonwealth, but he flatly refused continuation of partition.

De Valera, however, was not present at the treaty conference table; he remained in Dublin while other rebel leaders represented Ireland at the talks in London. The Irish delegates were finally convinced that a refusal of the Prime Minister's demand for the partition would cause all-out war. Without de Valera's approval, they signed a treaty agreeing to partition.

Some enraged I.R.A. leaders wanted to arrest the delegates and charge them with treason when they returned to Dublin. But most of the Irish people and the Catholic hierarchy were anxious for peaceful settlement. Over the strong opposition of de Valera and his Republican diehards, the treaty was approved by the Dail on January 7, 1922. Ireland was made a free state in the British Commonwealth. The six Ulster counties remained a province of the United Kingdom.

But the achievement of limited independence did not bring peace to Ireland. As soon as British troops were withdrawn from the land, a bitter civil war broke out between the pro-treaty Free State Government, headed by Collins and Griffith, and de Valera's Republicans.

THE first shots were fired on the morning of June 28 in the center of Dublin. Free Staters, using borrowed British artillery, mounted a bombardment on the historic Four Courts building, fortified as a Republican stronghold. As in the Easter Week battle, the fighting went on for eight days. Sixty men were killed and 300 wounded. While the Republicans were making a desperate last stand de Valera, who had rejoined his old I.R.A. unit, managed to escape from the city. Most of his soldiers were taken prisoner.

The loss of Dublin doomed the Republicans but the war dragged on for another year in the hills and small towns of the south and west. On August 12, Griffith died suddenly from strain and overwork, and 10 days later Collins was killed in a small skirmish on a country road in Cork. William Cosgrave took over the leadership of the Free State Government and refused a peace settlement offered by de Valera. When the Republicans abandoned the war on April 30, 1923, de Valera and the I.R.A. chiefs were forced to go into hiding.

Four months later Cosgrave called for a general election to strengthen his Government's position. From hiding, de Valera announced his candidacy for the Dail from his old constituency in Clare and declared that he would campaign in person. When he appeared at a rally in Ennis to make his opening campaign speech, he was arrested by Free State troops and imprisoned for almost a year. While in prison, he was elected in Clare, receiving twice as many votes as Eoin MacNeill, the Cosgrave party's candidate.

DE VALERA remained in jail until a general amnesty bill restored all Republicans to citizenship in 1924. He then broke with Sinn Fein in a dispute over the oath of allegiance to the British Crown, required under the Free State treaty for membership in the Irish Parliament, and formed his own Republican party, Fianna Fail (Warriors of Destiny), which became Cosgrave's strongest opposition.

The de Valera party was still faced, however, with the oath of allegiance problem. It was difficult to see how any political party could survive without representation in the Dail. But to gain a seat in the legislative body, a winning candidate had to swear allegiance to the King on a Bible and sign a statement of loyalty to him.

De Valera found a way around the obstacle by making one of the frequent abstract distinctions that have driven his political rivals to distraction. He decided that his Fianna Fail members would not really be taking the oath if they kept their hands off the Bible and announced while signing the allegiance statement that they were doing so only to gain admission to the Dail.

THUS the anti-oath Fianna Fail began to send members to Parliament and gained the power that eventually enabled de Valera to win control of the Government in 1932. One of his first official moves was to abolish the oath of allegiance. In 1936, after the abdication of King Edward VIII, de Valera and the Dail recognized George VI as head of the British Commonwealth, in which Ireland held membership; they denied him recognition, however, as King of Ireland. Under the new Irish constitution promulgated that year, Ireland was to have a President, elected by the people every seven years as a nonpolitical head of state. The real chief executive became a Prime Minister elected, as in Britain, by Parliament.

De Valera's party remained in control of the Government continuously in the years after 1932. His one regret during that period was the continued existence of partition. Since the 26 Catholic counties left the Commonwealth in 1949 to become the Republic of Eire, the chances of reunion with Protestant Ulster have seemed remoter than ever. The leadership of Fianna Fail was passed on to a younger veteran of the old I.R.A., Sean Lemass. In 1959 the Chief, as de Valera's followers call him, became the President of Ireland.

The President's handsome residence, in Dublin's Phoenix Park, was formerly the viceregal palace of the British Governor General. An Irish cab driver explained to one of de Valera's recent visitors that in the days of the governors general a cabbie, waiting for a passenger paying a call at the palace, would be served a sandwich and a bottle of ale.

"They don't do it any more, sir," the cab driver said. "But of course we are no longer as desperately hungry for a sandwich as we were back in those days when the British were here."

British troops round up rebels in Dublin in 1920 in front of the General Post Office (left), rebuilt after being destroyed in 1916.

Revolution, Civil War, and a Difficult Freedom

Although a yearning for home rule obsessed the Irish for centuries, they did not mount a full-scale rebellion until 1918, when Britain attempted to draft Irish soldiers into its Army. Indignant, Ireland claimed its independence. The next three years ran bloody with the carnage of guerrilla attacks and wholesale killing. In 1921 England granted Ireland self-determination—with conditions. The separation of six Northern counties from the 26 Southern counties was unacceptable to a sizable minority in the rest of the country. A 10-month-long civil war ensued. After a truce was signed, the nation fell into torpor. It was not until the early 1960s that vigorous Prime Minister Sean Lemass was able to awaken Ireland from its exhaustion and began to orient it toward international industrial society.

LEADERS of the rebellion, shown as they attended a hurling match in 1921, were *(left to right)* Arthur Griffith, Eamon de Valera, Laurence O'Neill and Michael Collins. Later de Valera broke with Griffith over partition.

BRUTAL REPRISAL was wrought by the English Black and Tans on the little town of Balbriggan on September 20, 1920. To avenge the death of a British soldier, the troops burned 25 houses and a factory to the ground.

MAGNETIC FIGURE, Constance Countess Markievicz confers with a labor-union leader, Cathal O'Shannon. Born to Irish Protestants and married to a Polish aristocrat, she fought in uniform for Irish independence.

REBELLION *provoked heroic defiance, wholesale reprisals, and the rising grief of a suppressed people*

REPUBLICAN TROOPS are inspected by Eamon de Valera in County Clare. Relying on guerrilla tactics, the Army staged ambushes and surprise attacks on British soldiers, then hid in households loyal to the Republic.

PATRIOTIC MARTYR, Terence MacSwiney, the Lord Mayor of Cork, was given a solemn funeral in 1920. Imprisoned in England for I.R.A. activities, he died after a 74-day hunger strike, exciting worldwide attention.

PROTESTING WOMEN, dressed in deep mourning and saying their rosaries, assembled with 20,000 other Dubliners on March 14, 1921 to pray for six Republican prisoners who were executed that day by the English.

LONG-AWAITED TREATY is ratified in Dublin on January 14, 1922, ending the conflict with England and establishing the Irish Free State in the British Commonwealth. Arthur Griffith, wearing glasses and seated in the middle of the bench at left center, was instrumental in negotiating the agreement and in gaining support for it in an Ireland sharply divided on the question.

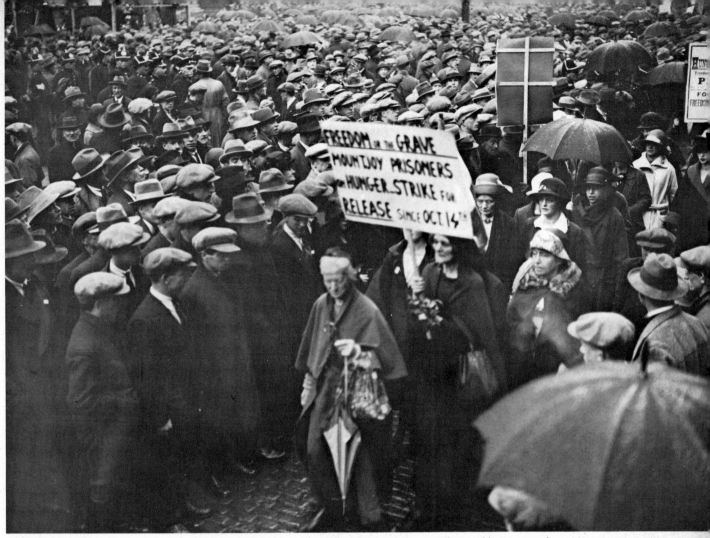

Demonstrators protest the imprisonment of anti-treaty Republicans by the Free Staters in 1923. The Republicans opposed partition.

ASCETIC HERO of The Troubles, Eamon de Valera was Ireland's Prime Minister for 21 years. He sought to return his nation to self-reliance and the language and customs of the past.

QUIET PROGRESSIVE, Sean Lemass became Prime Minister in 1959. Although a veteran of the I.R.A., he brought in bolder ideas and encouraged industry and foreign investment.

5

Devotion
to the
Church

AN American Communist returned from a tour
of Europe a few years ago and reported to
a fellow party member in New York the progress
of Marxism in the countries that he had visited.
He mentioned that Communism in Ireland was
forced to operate underground. "The Irish Communists won't identify themselves publicly as
members of the party," he explained, "because
they're afraid they may be excommunicated by
the Catholic Church."

Excommunication is indeed a stigma to be
avoided, even by a Communist, in the Republic of Ireland, one of the most solidly Roman
Catholic nations in the world. The partition of

1921 segregated most of Ireland's Protestants
under British government in the six Northern
counties of Ulster and left the area of the Republic with a population, now 2.8 million, that
is 95 per cent Catholic.

Although there are some 150,000 Protestants in the Republic, there are large areas
where there are no Protestants at all. Many
smaller towns have only two or three families in their dwindling Episcopal, Presbyterian and Methodist congregations. An Irishman observed recently that Sunday services at
the Episcopal cathedral in his community, well
filled 100 years ago, are now attended by "five

maiden ladies proudly hymning their defiance.''

The overwhelming dominance of Catholicism in Ireland leaves little, if any, separation between the Church and the state. As the writer Sean O'Faolain points out in a study of Irish Catholicism, the Church in Ireland does not need to resort to politics as it does in more secularized countries, such as Italy and France; it holds its power simply through the old bond of faith, unbroken in the Irish people since the Middle Ages. The Government, run by devout Catholics, is naturally influenced by the Church, and the average Irishman sees nothing alarming in this—after all, his own family life is also guided by the Church, and those politicians need the priests to keep an eye on them.

THE Irish Constitution guarantees religious freedom to all sects and creeds, but it acknowledges "the special position of the Holy Catholic Apostolic and Roman Church as the guardian of the Faith professed by the great majority of the citizens." The Government, on both the national and local levels, makes few moves affecting social welfare, education or health without the approval of the Catholic hierarchy, and any proposal strongly opposed by the Church would be in serious trouble. The Sinn Fein revolution against the British succeeded partly because it was not opposed by the bishops, and received outspoken support from some of them. The subsequent civil war waged by de Valera's antitreaty Republicans against the Free State failed partly because the clergy preached against it and denied the sacraments to the rebels.

All public elementary education in the country is under religious control—whether Catholic, Protestant or, in rare cases, Jewish. In every Catholic town the national, or public, elementary school attended by Catholic children is supervised by the local Catholic parish priest, as pastors are called in Ireland. He selects and hires the principal and approves the appointment of teachers. If nuns, priests or Catholic religious brothers teach in national schools, as they often do, the Government pays them the same salary it gives to lay teachers. Protestant children, however, are not required to attend Catholic-supervised schools. They go to a Government-supported school directed by the local Protestant minister. If there are not enough Protestant families in the community to require such a school, the children are provided with transportation to the nearest town that has one. Secondary schools, also subsidized by the Government, are in private hands, with many of the high schools and preparatory schools run by religious orders.

The Government also builds, with the ample funds of its Irish Hospital Sweepstakes lottery, hospitals, mental institutions and homes for the poor and aged that are staffed by members of religious orders. The dominating buildings in every sizable Irish town are the hospital and the Catholic church, and the dominating figure in local community life is the Catholic priest, "without whom," Sean O'Faolain writes, "any picture of modern Ireland is unthinkable."

The priest is deeply involved, directly or indirectly, in everything in his town, and he is an unofficial clan leader, consulted for advice and guidance not only in matters of family trouble but also in business or legal disputes, arguments over the ownership of livestock or land boundaries and squabbles about the selection of the local football team. In certain aspects of town and county government that concern social life, the priest's word is law. Without his consent, or at least his lack of opposition, it is impossible to open a new dance hall or saloon. It is due to the Church that Ireland has no night clubs, strip joints or drive-in movies.

YET for all his involvement in community life, and despite the fact that the local church is usually the town's social and recreation center, the Irish priest is placed on a pedestal that keeps him from mixing intimately and familiarly with his parishioners. Like a general in an army camp, he belongs to a special high caste. He is too respected and honored for his calling to be treated like other men. After he receives Holy Orders, even the members of his own family are in awe of him. It would be hard to imagine an Irish publisher bringing out a novel about an alcoholic priest, like the American writer Edwin O'Connor's *The Edge of Sadness*. Such a public discussion of human weakness in a man of God would be regarded as scandalous.

Members of the clergy in Ireland, in fact, are celebrities whose ecclesiastical ceremonies and public appearances are played up with pictures and headlines in the newspapers like the doings of movie or television stars in the United States. An indication of the high esteem for priests in Ireland is the fact that even in the smallest rural parishes the priests obtain their major support from privately paid tithes or a few annual offerings—and not from money obtained by passing collection baskets at Sunday Mass, the practice followed in parishes throughout the United States. Unlike the Catholic pastor in America, the Irish priest in charge of a larger parish is provided with a rectory where he lives alone, befitting his high station. His curates share another house.

THE public image of the Irish priest has changed considerably in recent years. Although Catholicism in Ireland is still sterner than the more relaxed variety found in Latin countries, the average modern cleric, with an Austin in his garage and a telephone and television set in his rectory, is much more tolerant and broadminded than the fire-breathing, small-town Irish pastor of 50 years ago. Many an Irishman who was young at the turn of the century has a vivid memory of the village priest hurrying along a road in the evening to chase home with his blackthorn stick the romantic young couple reported to be sitting on a gate. Even the most critical anticlerical Irish agree that those tyrannical guardians of their flocks have faded away with the clay pipe and the jaunting car, and that Ireland today is not the "priest-ridden" country that it used to be.

"The young people now won't stand for iron-handed moral dictatorship and the Irish Church is no longer inclined to exert it," a bishop in the midlands says. "The clergy in a thoroughly Catholic country like this one naturally has more authority than it has elsewhere, but we are well aware that authority can't be as rigid as it was in the time of Queen Victoria."

IRISH Catholics point to a number of recent expressions of public disagreement with the Church which they doubt could have happened 20 or 30 years ago. These instances range from the Government's support for General Assembly debate of the issue of Red China's admission to the United Nations down to a small but lively controversy in County Mayo that stirred up widespread interest. A group of Catholic teachers in a public school challenged the right of the local parish priest to appoint a member of a Catholic teaching order as principal of the school—instead of giving the job to one of them. To the disappointment of their admirers all over the country—including many members of the clergy—the laymen eventually compromised, accepting a raise in pay instead of the principalship. Technically they had given in—but the fact of their rebellion was significant.

The proposal late in 1963 to have Catholics take a pledge in Irish churches not to patronize immoral movies, as Catholics take the Legion of Decency oath in churches in the United States, met with such resistance that it was quietly dropped. Producers and writers in the Dublin theater and Irish television say that Church censorship is not at all as restraining as foreigners assume it to be. Jim Fitzgerald, director of *Stephen D.*, Hugh Leonard's dramatization of James Joyce's strongly anticlerical *Portrait of the Artist as a Young Man*, says that the play encountered not even a murmur of complaint when it was staged in Dublin. "But when we did it in London, the Lord High Chamberlain tried to chop it to pieces," he adds. Dubliners blame the notorious Irish censorship of books on the Government rather than on the clergy.

But if the Catholic Church in Ireland is more tolerant today than in the past, it is still too authoritarian for most Irish intellectuals and writers, whose ranks today are probably more filled with rebellious apostates than they were in James Joyce's day. The intellectuals complain that the modern Irish Church is more lenient with trivial and vulgar books and films than it is with those presenting challenging and nonconforming new ideas. Sean O'Faolain contends that there will be no common ground of discussion between Irish intellectual laymen and clergy as long as the priest continues to follow his traditional course of "applying to all intellectual ideas the test of their effect on the poor and the ignorant."

The Irish apostate, always a familiar figure on the Dublin scene, is seldom an atheist. Despite his violent anticlericalism, he cannot shake off the spirituality of his heritage. The most famous of all Irish apostates, Joyce, went to church every year on Holy Thursday and Good Friday long after he broke away from Catholicism. As he himself wrote, "it is a curious thing, do you know, how your mind is supersaturated with the religion in which you say you disbelieve."

LIKE almost everything in Ireland, the severe strictness of the old-time Catholic clergymen was rooted in historical events of the country's past. During the dark era of the anti-Catholic Penal Laws in the 18th Century, young Irishmen had to study for the priesthood on the Continent. In the early 1790s, the British Government became alarmed by the rise of Theobald Wolfe Tone's Irish Protestant revolutionary movement (see Chapter 3) and made hurried bids of appeasement to Irish Catholics in an effort to win their loyalty. One of these conciliatory moves was the establishment of the Catholic theological seminary at Maynooth in 1795.

Perhaps not entirely by accident, the faculty of the new college was staffed by refugees from the French Revolution, promonarchy theologians who hated Tone's republican ideas. Most of these theologians had been influenced by Jansenism—the rigid and gloomy doctrine,

denounced as Calvinistic by the Jesuits, that man is a helplessly doomed being who must endure punishing soul-searching and rigorous penance to prove his love of God. Mere faith and constant church-going, the Jansenists held, are not enough to win salvation. They attacked the Jesuits for granting absolution for sins leniently, and without assigning sufficient penance to the sinner.

Thanks to the influence of the French theologians at Maynooth, most of the Irish Catholic hierarchy sided with the British against Tone in the rebellion of 1798, and supported Prime Minister William Pitt's Act of Union. Their forbidding and stern Jansenist theory strongly flavored Irish Catholicism until it was finally officially discouraged in the middle of the 19th Century. The last vestiges of the doctrine have long since disappeared from Irish Catholicism, but the unusual devotion of the Irish people today to physically punishing religious pilgrimages possibly could be traced in part back to the old teaching at Maynooth that love of God must be demonstrated by harder acts than receiving the sacraments and going to daily Mass.

One of the most famous of these pilgrimages is the annual climbing of the 2,510-foot rocky slope of Croagh Patrick, the mountain overlooking Clew Bay in County Mayo where Saint Patrick fasted for 40 days and nights and where, according to legend, snakes and other reptiles fled from him. The pilgrims, usually numbering more than 60,000, make the climb before dawn on the last Sunday of July, many of them in bare feet. They stop during the ascent to pray, and finally attend Mass on the summit as the sun rises.

OTHER groups of pilgrims travel every day during the summer to Lough Derg, a lonely lake in Donegal where Saint Patrick is said to have seen a vision of Purgatory. A striking round-domed Romanesque basilica dedicated to the Saint rises like a mirage on a small island in the middle of the lake. The pilgrims arrive at noon, having fasted from the previous midnight, and spend the next 48 hours in prayer and meditation on the island. They remain awake for all of the first night and the next day, sustained only by a piece of dry bread and a cup of black tea, walking around the basilica without shoes while reciting rosaries and other prayers. On the second night they are allowed to sleep in hospices. When they leave the island on the morning of the third day, they fast again until they reach their homes. There are some old people who have made the strenuous annual pilgrimage to Lough Derg more than 50 times.

A NOTABLE new development in the modern Irish Catholic Church is the lay apostolic movement. The conservative hierarchy of the past openly discouraged laymen from reading theological works and from taking an active role in Church work. Until late in the 19th Century, most Catholics in Ireland were either illiterate in English or persons with limited education. It was felt that laymen lacking grounding in ecclesiastical learning might cause themselves only harmful confusion by delving too deeply into Church affairs and doctrine. But today many of the most dedicated crusaders for the Church in Ireland are men and women in lay organizations.

One of the strongest of these apostolic movements is the Legion of Mary, a volunteer force devoted to social work and spiritual rehabilitation that has spread all over the world since it was founded in Dublin in 1921. The Legion's active membership in Ireland is more than 100,000, and it sends teachers and lay missionaries to South America, Africa and Asia. The legionaries give a required number of hours each week to charitable service—trying to mend broken marriages, offering guidance to alcoholics and prostitutes, baby-sitting for working mothers, taking turns sleeping overnight in the homes of lone elderly people. The organization gives no material contributions —no food, clothing or money. "That's left to other agencies," explained Frank Duff, who founded the Legion and led it for many years. "We aim only at lifting people's spirit."

The Legion once undertook a mammoth job of spirit-lifting in a parish on the coast of Kerry that was slowly dying from apathy. Its young people were departing. There had been no births in the parish in five years. Hopelessness had settled like a cloud over the entire district; farmland was falling into neglect and homes were beginning to crumble, but the people made no move to help themselves. The worried parish priest appealed to the Legion.

"We went down there and noticed right away what the people themselves had long since failed to see," said Duff. "It was the most beautiful place on earth—the mountain and seaside scenery took your breath away."

With the financial help of the Irish Tourist Board, the Legion workers spent two years persuading the farmers in the parish to renovate their cottages and convert the area into a holiday resort. Agricultural experts showed the people how to profit from the mild Kerry climate by growing high-priced early vegetables. Soon every tourist home in the whole area was sold out for the two summer months, emigration had stopped and many young people were returning from abroad. "But more important, everybody is smiling and holding up his head again," said Duff.

N OT long ago an elderly priest was discussing the changed relationship between the modern Irish Catholics and the contemporary Irish Catholic Church. He mentioned with amusement that he had heard a popular story at a recent reunion of his class at Maynooth about a Galway clergyman who noticed a young girl from his parish sprawled on a beach wearing a very brief bikini. The priest sent the girl a note, asking her to wear a one-piece bathing suit. She returned a quick reply: "Which piece do you want me to take off?"

The old priest chuckled and said, "I can't imagine an Irish girl handing an answer like that to a priest 30 years ago. But then, of course, 30 years ago Irish girls didn't wear bikinis, now did they?"

A Rose Rooted in the Nation's Heart

A flower grows more heartily if every bloom but the topmost is sacrificed. Similarly, the Roman Catholic Church in Ireland, representing three fourths of the island's total population, reveals a surprising vigor in spite of, or perhaps because of, its centuries of travail. The Protestant cathedral and the Catholic cathedral on neighboring hills in Armagh symbolize the religious conflict over the island. Since the reign of Elizabeth I the struggle has raged, and under the 18th Century penal laws, when members of the Roman Church were denied all political and civil rights, the average Catholic learned to fight for his faith. The fervent and deep intimacy established long ago between the priest and his parishioner still prevails.

CATHOLIC ENTHRONEMENT by the apostolic nuncio (seated, far right) of Dr. William Conway (at the foot of the stairs) as primate of all Ireland occurs in Saint Patrick's Cathedral. Armagh has been a holy city since it was Saint Patrick's see.

*A PASTOR shows
a tender regard
for his charges
and a scholarly
sense of the past*

VISITING PARISHIONERS in a nearby village *(left)*, the Reverend Thomas A. Egan of Ballintubber, County Mayo, chats with one of the 138 families in his parish, near a castle built in the 17th Century.

INSPECTING MASONRY which has recently been unearthed, Father Egan surveys progress on his pet project, the restoration of Ballintubber Abbey *(background)*, where Mass has been offered for 750 years.

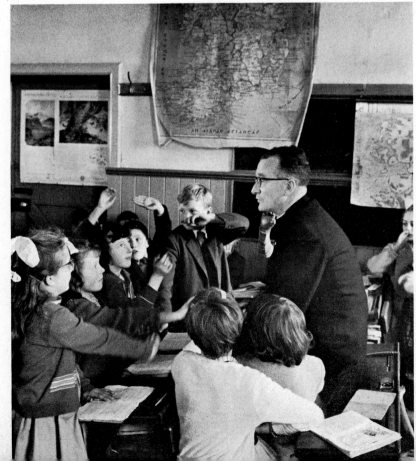

ANSWERING QUESTIONS raised by pupils in school, Father Egan fulfills one of the duties of all village priests, supervision of public education. Schools in the Irish Republic are allied with the Church.

IN A PRIVATE HOME Father Egan celebrates the Mass. During the centuries when Roman Catholics were persecuted in Ireland, the faithful held their services secretly in country cottages. In remembrance of those difficult times the Irish clergy was granted the unique privilege of holding "stations," or the offering of the Mass in the private homes of their parishioners.

WITH LIFTED HAND, Father Egan grants absolution to Joseph Walsh after hearing his confession in the house of Christy Finnerty, postman of the nearby village of Ballyglass.

THE MASS OVER, Mrs. Jack Hession, in whose home the service was held, serves Father Egan breakfast with the family (*right*). The dining room was redecorated for the occasion.

ECCLESIASTICAL CONFERENCE of Ireland's four archbishops and 24 bishops adjourns in the halls of Saint Patrick's College, established in 1795 at Maynooth, County Kildare.

SOLEMN ORDINATION introduces 48 seminarians into the priesthood at Saint Patrick's College. As the students prostrate themselves, a bishop prays before ordaining them priests.

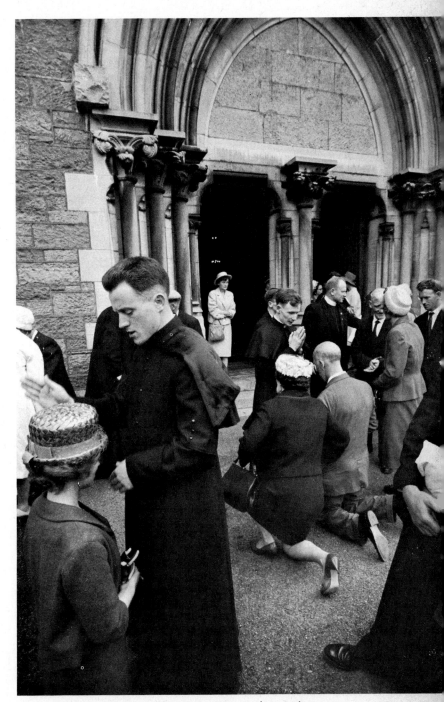

THE PRIESTHOOD, *a calling*
to quiet action and patient service,
begins with a ceremony full of emotion

FIRST BLESSINGS given by the new priests are bestowed upon members of their familes. The greatest seminary in Ireland, Saint Patrick's has also been increasing its lay student enrollment.

87

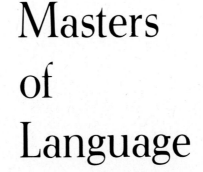

6

Masters
of
Language

FOR a small and poor nation, Ireland has produced an astonishing number of the world's great writers. Many of the leading literary figures before 1900 were Irish or of Irish background—Jonathan Swift, Oliver Goldsmith, George Berkeley, William Congreve, Oscar Wilde. Then, in the next 25 years came a spectacular outburst of writing talent from Ireland that gave the English literature of the 20th Century its best dramatists, George Bernard Shaw, John Millington Synge and Sean O'Casey; its best poet, William Butler Yeats; and the giant of modern novelists, James Joyce, who has been described as the greatest master of the English language since Milton.

This sparkling array of Irish authors, which also included George Moore, Æ (George Russell), James Stephens, Liam O'Flaherty, Lady Augusta Gregory and Frank O'Connor, emerged suddenly to a position of leadership in the literary world of the new century because they filled a sorely felt need of their time. In the 1890s, literature generally was divided into two extreme schools of writing. One was represented by the murky, romantic lyricism of the French poet Stéphane Mallarmé and the dramas of Oscar Wilde, ornate, artificial and detached from the troublesome problems of life. At the opposite, distant pole was the realism of the plays of Henrik Ibsen of Norway and the naturalism of the novels of Émile Zola of France. There was a yearning for writing that would close the wide gap between these two extremes, for the creation of poems, plays and novels dealing with reality and real people, but in rich and colorful language.

The Irish writers were well-equipped to satisfy that need. They had poetry; they had humor; they had a hard realism. They reflected the hopes and dreams of common people because their literary movement was linked chronologically and spiritually to the rise of Irish nationalism and the rebellion against Britain. Even the writers themselves were bound up in the nationalist cause. James Joyce's first published piece of writing, composed when he was only nine years old, was *Et Tu, Healy*, a diatribe against a political betrayer of Charles Stewart Parnell, the Home Rule leader. A Parnell admirer, Joyce's father had it privately printed and proudly handed it out to his friends. William Butler Yeats wrote with deep feeling of the Easter Week uprising of 1916. Two poets prominent in the literary movement, Padraic Pearse and Joseph Mary Plunkett, were executed for their leading parts in that revolt. Sean O'Casey was one of the original organizers of the Irish Citizen Army.

Part of the nationalist movement was the Gaelic League, founded in 1893 to revive Ireland's interest in the Gaelic language and the forgotten native literature of the Middle Ages. This patriotic effort had far-reaching effects. The unearthing of the heroic epics composed by ancient Celtic poets stirred in Yeats, the real father of the modern Irish literary revival, a new appreciation of his native country's heritage, and turned him back to Ireland from the studies of William Blake and theosophy that

---

IRISH AUTHORS' NAMES

Below is a guide to the pronunciation of the names of some of the more prominent Irish authors who are mentioned in this chapter.

Brendan Behan: Brendan "Bee'-an."
Sean O'Casey: "Shawn" O'Casey.
Sean O'Faolain: "Shawn O'Faylawn."
Padraic Pearse: "Paw-drick Pierce."
John Millington Synge: John Millington "Sing."
William Butler Yeats: William Butler "Yates."

---

he had been pursuing in London. Yeats took another look at the Sligo country, where he had spent much of his youth, and visited the bleak Aran Islands off the western coast of Ireland. He became engrossed in the possibilities for literary material in the dignity, colorful language and rough struggle for existence of the peasants in the west of Ireland. In 1896, Yeats came across Synge studying Racine and other French dramatists in Paris, the accepted course in that period for young men with literary ambitions. He convinced Synge that there was more to be gained from a study of people on the Aran Islands than from reading in French libraries.

"That meeting of two Irishmen in Paris, agreeing that the life of those most remote and barren Aran Islands was the full material for literature, is a parable that marks the final stage of growth of the Irish mind," as the author Sean O'Faolain wrote later. "It was an entirely new thing for men to realize the full and complete dignity of the simplest life of the simplest people. Once they had acknowledged that then they were free to do anything they liked with it in literature—treat it naturalistically, fantastically, romantically, see it in any light they chose. They had conquered their material by accepting it."

Out of this realization and acceptance came such plays as Synge's *Riders to the Sea* and *The Playboy of the Western World*, both first produced at the Abbey Theatre in Dublin. The Abbey, in which Yeats and Lady Augusta Gregory were important figures, brought a fresh breath of real life to theater audiences long jaded by the fashionable comedies of Wilde, the problem plays of Sir Arthur Wing Pinero, and the flashy melodramas of Dion Boucicault, an Irishman who had enjoyed success in London. The extraordinary freshness, as George Bernard Shaw pointed out approvingly, was due to Yeats's and Lady Gregory's holding ruthlessly "to my formula of making the audience believe that real things were happening to real people."

Shaw himself, who was furiously busy in London writing plays, was no slavish follower of his own "formula." His characters speak with a superhuman articulateness and wit, and they are sometimes more embodiments of an idea than believable human beings. But the ideas, frequently paradoxical and outrageous, flash and crackle, and the characters carom off one another with such vigor that they frequently seem more than alive. Especially in such turn-of-the-century plays as *Candida, Arms and the Man, Caesar and Cleopatra* and *Man and Superman,* Shaw performed the extraordinary feat of turning "problem plays"—dramas designed to preach one of the author's social doctrines—into delightful and satisfying theater. Starting with an idea, such as the notion that munitions makers do the world more good by providing employment than the Salvation Army can ever do with Christian uplift and soup kitchens, Shaw so effectively illustrated the idea with vivid characters and lively scenes in *Major Barbara* that he succeeded in turning propaganda into something very close to great art.

MUCH of the attraction of the Abbey Theatre in its great early days between 1904 and the 1920s was attributed to Yeats's stern dictum, gladly followed by such dramatists as Synge and O'Casey, that the most realistic plays should employ the magic language of poetry. Synge wrote in an introduction to *The Playboy of the Western World* his disapproval of the practice of Ibsen and Zola of dealing with reality "in joyless and pallid words." Every speech in a good play, he contended, should be as fully flavored as a nut or an apple.

To Yeats, the theater was an important medium of artistic expression, but his own main function as a writer was in lyric poetry. His technical skill and his talent for combining conversational ease of expression and noble emotion within the strict framework of rhyme and poetic form was so rare that many modern critics now consider him not only the greatest poet of the century but perhaps the greatest since Elizabethan times.

Unlike such lyric poets as John Keats or Dylan Thomas, who died young, or as Wordsworth, who faded in his middle years, Yeats improved with age. Much of his best work was written in his fifties and sixties. A woolly romanticist in his youth, he moved on to stern, symbolic realism dealing with "the chaos of the world," full of powerful intensity and chilling images, and far more exalted than the pleasant verse with which some readers associate him:

> *I will arise and go now, and go to Innisfree,*
> *And a small cabin build there, of clay*
> *   and wattles made;*
> *Nine bean rows will I have there, a hive*
> *   for the honey bee,*
> *And live alone in the bee-loud glade . . .*

Such lyricism stands in strong contrast to lines like these, composed in later life:

> *Turning and turning in the widening gyre*
> *The falcon cannot hear the falconer;*
> *Things fall apart; the centre cannot hold;*
> *Mere anarchy is loosed upon the world,*
> *The blood-dimmed tide is loosed, and everywhere*
> *The ceremony of innocence is drowned;*
> *The best lack all conviction, while the worst*
> *Are full of passionate intensity.*

Yeats and Synge, like Shaw, Lady Gregory and George Moore, were from upper-class Anglo-Irish Protestant families. Before the turn of the century, most Catholics in Ireland were too underprivileged culturally, as well as economically and socially, to nourish an interest in the creative arts. The rise of James Joyce to literary greatness from an impoverished Catholic home in Dublin is a striking example of inborn genius triumphing over harsh and discouraging environment, almost like a rose blooming from an ash heap.

As a youngster, Joyce was not exposed within his family or at school to any intellectual stimulation that might have urged him to become a precedent-breaking experimenter in modern writing. His mother was a devoutly religious woman with no consuming interest in intellectual matters; his father was a music lover and a witty raconteur. At the local Jesuit schools, Joyce was taught by conventional and dogmatic classicists. Whatever knowledge he had of contemporary writing was gained from unguided reading on his own.

Yet when he was 18 years old, an obscure student at University College, Dublin, Joyce read Henrik Ibsen's new play, *When We Dead Awaken*, in its original Norwegian text (he had taught himself that language just to be able to read Ibsen), and wrote a long critical essay on the play which was immediately accepted by the *Fortnightly Review*, the most important literary periodical in London at that time. Ibsen was so impressed by the understanding of his work shown in the article—rare in the English-speaking world of 1900—that he wrote a message of gratitude to his English translator, William Archer, which Archer passed on to Joyce.

Like Shaw before him, and many young Irish writers after him, Joyce left Ireland at an early age to spend the rest of his life in self-exile abroad. The atmosphere of Dublin 70 years ago, much more narrowly provincial and stiffly conventional than it is nowadays, was stifling to a highly individual and nonconforming artist. Explaining his own departure from Dublin at the age of 20, Shaw once wrote, "Every Irishman who felt that his business in life was on the higher planes of the cultural professions felt that he must have a metropolitan domicile and an international culture: that is, he felt that his first business was to get out of Ireland."

SHAW'S Irish upbringing and Irish point of view is often cited, however, as a main factor behind his success as a London critic and dramatist. Joyce's Irishness is an even more dominating force in his literary work because in all four of the books that made him famous

—*Dubliners*, *A Portrait of the Artist as a Young Man*, *Ulysses* and *Finnegans Wake*—he never left Ireland. Although he lived in France, Austria and Switzerland during his creative years, all of his stories and novels take place in the Dublin of his youth.

JOYCE bitterly resented his inability to see his books published in Dublin during his lifetime. His first book, *Dubliners,* a collection of ironic and acid short stories, was rejected by Irish printers because they feared its references to living Dubliners and believed that one disrespectful mention of King Edward VII might cause legal repercussions. *Ulysses* and *A Portrait of the Artist as a Young Man* were ruled out on the grounds of immorality and impiety. Never formally censored, *Finnegans Wake* was too difficult to be a popular book in Ireland or in any country. After the suppression of *Dubliners,* Joyce wrote a long protest in doggerel, which he called *Gas from a Burner,* describing Ireland as:

> *This lovely land that always sent*
> *Her writers and artists to banishment*
> *   and in a spirt of Irish fun*
> *Betrayed her own leaders, one by one.*
> *'Twas Irish humour, wet and dry,*
> *Flung quicklime into Parnell's eye . . .*
> *O Ireland my first and only love*
> *Where Christ and Caesar are hand in glove!*

For all his indignation, Joyce remained obsessed with Ireland until his death in Zurich in 1941; he eagerly begged for its latest news and gossip and looked back on Dublin with admiration. In a letter to his brother, Stanislaus Joyce, he once expressed regret that he had not written in *Dubliners* of the attractiveness of his native city. "I have not been just to its beauty," Joyce said of Dublin, "for it is more beautiful naturally, in my opinion, than what I have seen of England, Switzerland, France, Austria and Italy."

Joyce's writings are often assumed to be too obscure for an average reader. Actually, the clear and hard-hitting stories in *Dubliners* are easier to read than much of the fiction now published in *The New Yorker*. *A Portrait of the Artist as a Young Man*, Joyce's account of his own soul-struggle as he was seeking his course in life as an independent artist, is not a difficult book. He begins to navigate more murky and puzzling depths in *Ulysses* when he explores the streams of his characters' conscious thinking, and then goes into still deeper waters in *Finnegans Wake*, a probing of one man's unconscious and sleeping mind.

In *Ulysses*, which he modeled after Homer's *Odyssey*, Joyce tells a simple story of one day in the lives of two men in Dublin. The day happens to be June 16, 1904. One of the two men, Stephen Dedalus, is Joyce himself at the age of 22, after the death of his mother summoned him from literary exile in Paris. He is at loose ends, isolated, alone, seeking a father. The other man, Leopold Bloom, a Jew and therefore an alien among the Irish, is the wandering Odysseus, or Ulysses, in search not of home, as in the *Odyssey*, but of a son. A third prominent character is Bloom's lusty wife, Molly. Stephen is the intellect, Bloom is Everyman, both sensual and thoughtful, and Molly is the flesh and the earth.

The book follows Stephen and Bloom along their separate ways through the day, showing not only their encounters with a great gallery of other colorful, comic and tragic characters but their innermost fleeting thoughts and impressions. Joyce divides their travels into a series of episodes, each designed after a scene in the *Odyssey* and each written in a different style. The book includes parodies, allegories, dialogues, stream of consciousness soliloquies, symbolism and catechetical questions and answers. The two men meet at night in a Dublin hospital and proceed to a brothel. Bloom takes Stephen to his home for a cup of cocoa; the son finds the father and the father finds the son. Discovering Bloom—Everyman —Stephen discovers mankind and sees and understands what he himself is going to be, a mature man, no longer imprisoned in a cell of childish ego and intellectual pride.

Unlike other novelists, Joyce does not use the passage of time to show changes and development of characters. Like a dramatist or a screen writer, he presents his people and scenes in the present tense. The men and women in *Ulysses*, like the characters of Shakespeare, come before the reader fully formed and bursting with life, and the sounds, smells and feelings of the June day in the Dublin of 1904 rise from the printed pages with the reality of a color movie. Because it uses words to reproduce visual and audible as well as mental sensations, *Ulysses* baffles the quick and casual reader, but many students of literature agree that it is probably the greatest book of our time.

Joyce's last work, *Finnegans Wake*, is harder going because it takes up where *Ulysses* leaves off and tries to follow a man's mind through a night of sleep. Just as an unconscious mind makes no attempt to explain its jumbled images and thoughts, Joyce leaves the meanings of his tangled dreamworld's words and phrases undeciphered. The title of the book itself is a play on words; one of its interpretations is "Finn Again Awake," meaning that the heroism of Finn MacCool should return to Ireland.

For all its difficult shaded meanings and verbal puzzles, *Finnegans Wake* is a tour de force of psychological insight expressed in a poetic

---

THE FAMOUS TRIAL OF "ULYSSES"

James Joyce's *Ulysses* has a special significance for Americans, for it was the subject of one of the most celebrated court decisions in U.S. jurisprudence, the Woolsey Decision of 1933. Shortly after the novel was published in Paris in 1922, it was banned in England and America. In 1933 a U.S. publishing house determined to bring the matter into court and, if successful, to publish an American edition. The decision, rendered by Judge John M. Woolsey, is a masterpiece of brevity and cool logic, and has remained a cornerstone of subsequent rulings on censorship. Woolsey said, in effect, that even though there are repeated frank references to sex and repeated use of four-letter words in *Ulysses*, this normally offensive material is there as a necessary part of Joyce's "sincere and serious" attempt to render fully and honestly the way people act and think.

prose that continually fascinates creative writers. Thornton Wilder, the American playwright and novelist, devotes part of every day to a study of the book. The famed Welsh lyric poet, Dylan Thomas, replied when asked what he thought of *Finnegans Wake*, "Why read anything else?"

Ireland today is no longer the center of literature that it was when Yeats, Synge and Joyce were producing a body of writing which, in the opinion of Harry Levin, the distinguished Harvard professor of comparative literature, defies comparison for intermingling of imaginative expression and closeness to familiar experience without going back to the Elizabethans. Sean O'Casey, the self-styled "Green Crow" whose *Juno and the Paycock* and *The Plough and the Stars* were among the most powerful plays produced by Yeats in the Abbey Theatre, moved to England in the 1920s and lived and wrote there for the rest of his life. The best-known Irish prose writers still close to the Irish scene are Liam O'Flaherty and Sean O'Faolain, versatile men of letters who are both regarded as outstanding short-story creators.

A NOTABLE figure in the avant-garde theater of recent years has been Irish-born Samuel Beckett, a disciple and associate of Joyce, whose *Waiting for Godot, Endgame* and *Krapp's Last Tape,* all highly acclaimed in the European theater, were originally written in French. Later translated into English by Beckett himself, all have certain qualities which might be called Irish—gaiety and bleakness, humor and despair—and convictions which seem alien to Irish writing: the beliefs, for example, that man is miserable, that knowledge is unattainable, and that both facts are wildly hilarious.

The contemporary Irish author and dramatist with more international fame than any of his living compatriots was Brendan Behan, who died in 1964 at the age of 41. Behan often interrupted a performance of one of his plays by appearing on the stage in person to address several hundred well-rounded, extemporaneous

sentences to the audience. Critics have been hard-pressed to categorize his harum-scarum theatrical writing. "In Brendan Behan's tremendous new play," Kenneth Tynan wrote in *The Observer* of London after the opening of *The Quare Fellow*, "language is out on a spree, ribald, dauntless and spoiling for a fight."

A NOTHER important playwright, in the opinion of Dubliners, is Hugh Leonard, whose theatrical adaptation of Joyce's *A Portrait of the Artist as a Young Man*, entitled *Stephen D.*, won critical acclaim. Leonard's play was produced in Dublin at the Gate Theatre rather than the Abbey, now a national theater subsidized by the Government. The Government, according to Irish theatrical people, has done the Abbey no good.

"Yeats would turn over in his grave if he could see what they're putting on," a Dublin theater and television director says. "Mostly what Americans would call soap operas. Cliché-type plays about nice middle-class families with the prodigal son returning to the church and signing up with the Legion of Mary at the final curtain. We think we're doing exciting things in the theater here in Dublin—but none of them are taking place at the Abbey".

Dublin has its quota of modern painters, but its only notable 20th Century artist was Jack B. Yeats, the poet's brother, who died in 1957 and whose work—mostly paintings done in Galway and Mayo—is not well known because he refused to allow most of it to be reproduced. Nor do the Irish figure prominently in modern music. In an attempt to encourage the creative arts, the government passed a law in 1969 that exempts any creative artist living in Ireland from paying income tax.

Language is the forte of the Irish—written, spoken or shouted. They are proud of a French critic's comment on the author of *Ulysses* and *Finnegans Wake:* "Joyce traces the language to its source, where the spoken word and thought are intimately bound together. With Joyce, language is not the vehicle and the means of thought. It is the thought itself."

Wearing a hat to shield his painfully weak eyes, James Joyce poses for a famous portrait taken by Berenice Abbott in Paris in 1928.

Artists Constructing the Conscience of Their Race

In Joyce's 1916 novel, *A Portrait of the Artist as a Young Man,* the hero proclaims that he will "forge . . . the uncreated conscience of my race." Irish artists of this century have, it can be said, done just that. Raising the lilting Irish idiom to poetic heights, they have ennobled the English language. And holding before their own people the cruel mirror of realism, showing every folly and vice, they have helped, as only great artists can, a people to know itself and become strong.

MASTERFUL WRITERS have been in the vanguard of drama and poetry, making their nation a major force in 20th Century literature

WILLIAM BUTLER YEATS, since his death in 1939, has been increasingly considered the century's greatest lyric poet. Born to an old Irish family in 1865, Yeats early determined to become a poet, but did his best work after the age of 45 when he had developed a style unequaled for its combination of ease and power.

JOHN MILLINGTON SYNGE, shown in a contemporary drawing *(below)*, is best known for his comic drama, *The Playboy of the Western World*, but he also wrote a poetic tragedy, *Riders to the Sea*, and two superb short farces. Although he died at 37, Synge had succeeded in making an evocative language of Irish peasant speech.

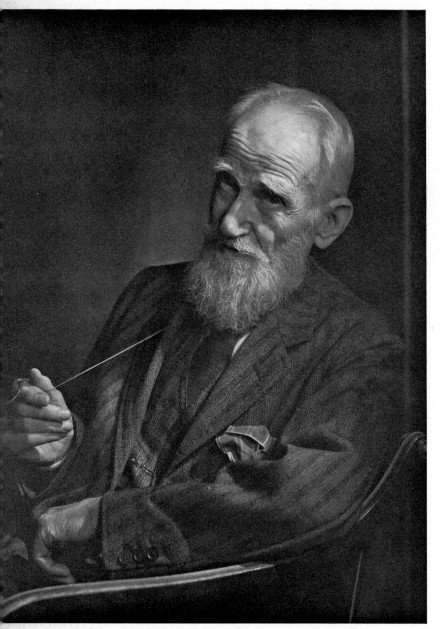

GEORGE BERNARD SHAW used a flashing Irish wit to amuse the audience while his plays drove home hard and unpalatable truths about mankind. The long prefaces he added to most of his plays are masterpieces of English polemical writing. Born in Dublin in 1856, Shaw remained vigorous until his death at 94 in 1950.

SEAN O'CASEY, long self-exiled in England, remained a sharp critic of what he considered the bigotry and hypocrisy of his native Ireland. A patriot during The Troubles, he later lashed the shiftlessness of the Irish in such satiric plays as *Juno and the Paycock*. He completed an absorbing six-volume autobiography in 1954.

SAMUEL BECKETT'S plays and novels portray a decaying world with a grim humor reminiscent of his Irish predecessor Jonathan Swift. Living in Paris, Beckett *(right)* is best known for his cryptic plays, such as *Waiting for Godot* and *Endgame*. For his contribution to letters, he was awarded the Nobel Prize for Literature in 1969.

PAINTERS capture in fresh colors the country's gaiety and romantic loneliness

BELOVED PATRIARCH of modern Irish painting, Jack B. Yeats, brother of poet W. B. Yeats, executes a sketch at his easel. Yeats painted hundreds of vivid scenes of Ireland before his death in 1957.

NOTED CONTEMPORARY, Patrick Collins pauses in his paneled studio. Collins, one of a score of able painters now working in Ireland, has had his work exhibited in Dublin, London and New York.

TURBULENT ENERGY pervades Yeats's 1930 oil, *The Horse Lover*. Yeats's favorite subjects included horses in action, the vivid confusion of country fairs and the ever-changing sky of western Ireland.

WISTFUL MELANCHOLY seems to dominate the misty landscape of Collins' *Country Road*. Many of Collins' paintings are romantic evocations of a lonely countryside or a deserted back street at twilight.

7

The Northern Irish

THE partition of Ireland into the 26 counties of the Republic and the United Kingdom's six counties of the North has long thrown a shadow of frustration and a deep sense of loss across the entire island. "One of the few occasions nowadays when Irishmen from both sides of the border get together to cheer the same team is at one of our international rugby matches," a Dublin newspaper editor said recently. "Ulstermen and Republicans are both wearing the same green jerseys and playing side by side against Wales or England. Perhaps I'm a sentimental fool, but when that crowd rises up and roars, 'Come on, *Ireland!*',

and you know it *is* Ireland that they're cheering —not the 26 counties or the six counties, but all of Ireland—well, I think of what could have been if it wasn't for that blasted treaty in 1921, and the tears come to my eyes and I get all choked up."

Yet despite the sense of loss, the antagonisms between divided Ireland's Catholic majority in the Republic and the Fundamental Protestants of the North are old, deep and broad—and involve more than religious differences. The Irish were at odds with each other over the question of allegiance to Britain long before Henry VIII's break with Rome pinned identifying badges of

Catholicism and Protestantism on the two opposing factions. As the struggle went on after the Reformation, religion became so intertwined with politics that in today's sequel—the battle over the partition—it is hard to tell where one leaves off and the other begins. While many observers in Ireland believe that the conflict between the North and the South is mainly religious, the Northern Irish disagree. They say the differences between them are basic.

"Aside from our Protestantism, we Orange Irish are an entirely different kind of people from the other Irish," says a man in Belfast. "We have a different racial background, different temperament, different outlook. We have too little in common with the Republicans to share a government with them."

THE Northern Presbyterians and Church of Ireland Episcopalians, along with a few Methodists and Baptists are sometimes referred to as Orange Irish because their ancestors supported the victorious Protestant King William of Orange against the Roman Catholic James II at the Battle of the Boyne in 1690. Many of them are members of the Orange Order, a Masonic-like organization dedicated to Irish Protestantism. The Battle of the Boyne is commemorated annually in Ulster, and its anniversary, celebrated on July 12, is an occasion for parades and speeches declaring Ulster's allegiance to Great Britain and the British Crown.

The banners that deck the Belfast streets on July 12 mention in their patriotic slogans the year 1912 and a document called the Solemn League and Covenant more often, however, than they recall 1690 and the Battle of the Boyne. "The Solemn League and Covenant," cries one sign on a street corner near the giant Harland & Wolff shipyards, "is a perpetual certificate of the indissoluble marriage of Ulster and the Crown."

The Covenant, as it is usually called, was Orange Ireland's expression of its opposition to the authority of Green Ireland, drawn up in 1912 by Sir Edward Carson, the Ulster Unionist leader, and signed by some 220,000 Ulstermen.

Earlier in that year Lord Asquith, the British Prime Minister, had offered Ireland a Home Rule bill that would have established an Irish parliament in Dublin with jurisdiction over purely Irish affairs. Carson's Covenant declared that if such a parliament were convened, Ulster would refuse to recognize it. Carson and his Unionist party, so-called because its members favored the continuation of Ireland's union with the United Kingdom, also formed an armed auxiliary and threatened to resist Home Rule with force.

THIS led to the break between Ulster and the rest of Ireland that later prompted the British Prime Minister David Lloyd George to propose a revised Home Rule bill, now known to the Irish as the Partition Act. It called for two parliamentary governments, one for the six northeastern counties of Ulster and the other in Dublin for the rest of the country, and it provided for an all-Ireland governing council in which the six Ulster counties would have as much authority as the other 26 counties combined. Sinn Fein's refusal to accept the partition bill was one of the reasons for the nationalists' armed rebellion against Britain in 1919-1920.

When that rebellion ended in the treaty conferences in London in 1921, David Lloyd George threatened Eamon de Valera's plenipotentiaries with all-out war if the partition were not accepted. To de Valera's dismay, Lloyd George won his demand. Thus the six Ulster counties remained in the United Kingdom with provincial self-government, while the other 26 counties first became the Irish Free State associated with the British Commonwealth and later broke off completely to form an independent Republic. Carson, the father of the partition, stands today commemorated in a bronze statue in front of the magnificent Northern Ireland Parliament building at Stormont, on the outskirts of Belfast.

The Parliament building, standing on high ground overlooking a mile of beautifully landscaped lawn, is one of the most impressive government capitols in the world, but its authority is limited to local matters. All major decisions concerning foreign policy, defense, tariffs and income taxes are made in the British Parliament at Westminster. Stormont can impose taxes only on motor vehicles, entertainment and deaths. "Technically the Westminster Parliament is free to legislate for Northern Ireland as if there were no local parliament," the Government information service at Stormont says. However, in practice Stormont's authority within its own field is never challenged, and it is able to legislate on matters of education, social welfare, labor and trade. Income taxes collected by the British Government are turned over to the Government of Northern Ireland, which budgets and spends the money in accordance with its own needs.

As evidence of their difference from the Green Irish, the Orange people point out that Ulster is the only part of Ireland that has been industrialized for the past century. They deny, as the Southern Irish claim, that they were given this economic opportunity by the British because of their Protestantism. It is a matter of racial character, they say, rather than religious discrimination.

THE Ulster Protestants have little of the ancient Irish Celtic ancestry. Their forefathers were the Scottish Presbyterian and English Anglican colonists brought to the Ulster Plantation settlement after the flight of the O'Neill and O'Donnell earls into exile in 1607. They also have a sprinkling of French Protestant ancestry from Huguenot weavers who came from the Continent and started Ulster's textile industry in the 17th Century. This background, the Northern Irish insist, gave them a natural inclination for mechanical work and for the organization of factory routine. They believe that these talents are not shared by the undisciplined and impractical Celts.

There is no doubt that the Northern Irish Protestants are a different breed from their Catholic neighbors of older native stock. They are more serious and stolid. Their capital city of Belfast, which quickly grew from a small town to a crowded manufacturing center in the 19th Century, has a stern Victorian look unlike that of any of the older cities in the South. Large areas of the northeast corner of Ireland—only 21 miles across the water at one point from Scotland —have a heavily Scottish flavor, and the people speak with a Scottish brogue, using words like "aye," "wee" and "bairn."

NORTHERN Ireland, as the Government of the United Kingdom calls the six Irish counties, and Ulster, as the British territory north of the border is familiarly known, are both misnomers. The area does not include the most northern part of Ireland, Donegal, and it does not cover all of the old province of Ulster. Donegal, Cavan and Monaghan are the three old Ulster counties that Carson's Unionists never seriously claimed. The Unionists agreed that these counties on the western and southern edges of the original province of Ulster would be better left outside. Their solidly Catholic and Nationalist populations would have endangered the majority control that the Orange Unionist Party hoped to wield—and has wielded —in the provincial Government of Northern Ireland established in 1921.

A contentious issue that has often been raised by the Republicans of the South against the partition is the claim that two other Ulster counties, Fermanagh and Tyrone, are also too Catholic and Nationalist to belong to the British. Other areas which are predominantly Catholic within the partitioned province are the southern parts of Armagh and Down counties and a large section of the county of Derry (renamed Londonderry by the British) that includes the city of Derry. Although the Protestants outnumber the Catholics by 2 to 1 in the six counties' total population of about 1.5 million, most of this two-thirds majority is closely concentrated around Belfast. Yet the Unionists, controlled by Protestants, manage to dominate local government in all six counties, and they occupy 36 of the 52 seats in the provincial Parliament's House of

Commons and 18 of the 26 seats in its Senate. All but two of the 12 of Northern Ireland's members of the United Kingdom's House of Commons at Westminster are Unionists.

For years the Unionists held political control in Catholic Nationalist counties by gerrymandering, the arranging of constituencies so that the minority party can elect more officeholders than the opposing majority. A study of gerrymandering in Ulster shows that in the 1954-1955 city council election, the city of Derry, with 31,620 Nationalist and 18,479 Unionist voters, was divided into three wards. Most of the Nationalists were crammed into one ward that could elect only eight of the city's 20 councilors. In the other two wards, which had 12 council seats between them, much smaller contingents of Unionists won by safe margins.

But their opposition's disorganization has also helped the Unionists to maintain control. Since many anti-Unionists are republican and do not believe in representation in Britain they have not sought election to Westminster. Until 1969 about half of the seats to the provincial Parliament were uncontested by the Nationalists.

RELIGIOUS ill will has had a substantial effect on hiring practices. In 1933 Sir Basil Brooke, later Lord Brookeborough, Unionist Prime Minister of Northern Ireland, made an appeal in a speech to Orange employers, asking them to hire "good Protestant lads and lassies." For many years Catholic workers had difficulties obtaining jobs in Belfast's two biggest industrial plants, the Harland & Wolff shipyards and the affiliated Short Brothers & Harland aircraft factory. Although religious discrimination has been slowly disappearing in recent years, the unemployment rate remains higher among Catholic workers than among Protestant.

Unemployment has continued to plague Belfast in recent years because shipbuilding and linen weaving, the city's main sources of jobs, have both been in a steady decline. The shipyards that hired 18,000 workers in 1960—more than 10 per cent of all industrial employees in Ulster that year—provided only 9,000 jobs in 1969.

Northern Ireland's 1969 unemployment rate was seven per cent, compared to 2.5 per cent in the rest of the United Kingdom. Meanwhile the population, unlike that of emigration-hit Republican Ireland, is showing a constant increase.

To fight unemployment and to overcome its dependence on shipbuilding and the linen trade, Northern Ireland is campaigning to attract new and more diversified industries. It offers a skilled labor force that its neighbor to the south cannot match, Government industrial grants covering about 50 per cent of plant-building costs, and well-developed ports at Belfast, Derry and Larne. As still another attraction for industry, the Government has created "growth centers" where manufacturing is combined with modern housing in new towns like Craigavon.

AMONG the new industrial plants in Ulster are several bearing impressive British, German and American names. Among them are Courtaulds, Imperial Chemicals, Monsanto, Berkshire Knitting, Hughes Tool, Hoechst, Bausch & Lomb and Grundig. Near Belfast the British Petroleum Company is operating Northern Ireland's first oil refinery, and Michelin of France is making tires from synthetic rubber produced by a Du Pont factory in Derry, providing employment for more than 4,000 people.

Despite its self-consciousness about unemployment, Northern Ireland carries on a foreign trade several times as large as that of the Republic —with about half as many people to support. Moreover, only 10 per cent of the Ulster work force is engaged in farming; the comparable figure in the Republic is about 30 per cent.

The partition has brought Ireland economic misery in many small but acutely painful ways. Laborers and white-collar workers from the Republic, welcomed in other parts of the United Kingdom, cannot obtain jobs in Northern Ireland without securing working permits that are difficult to get. The border barrier cuts across the middle of several market districts, depriving towns on both sides of trade that they formerly depended on for employment. The border, of course, also cuts Ulster off from the nearest market for its goods. For Ulster, however, there are advantages in partition. Northern Ireland's standard of living is substantially higher than that of the Republic, and social welfare benefits in the United Kingdom are more extensive.

SO much disparity and antagonism has fostered strife in Ulster for decades. One of the most appalling clashes between Orange and Catholic Nationalist Irish—a three-day riot in Belfast in July 1920, in which 18 people were killed and 200 injured—started as a demonstration in the shipyards against Sinn Fein. Belfast was in the throes of one of its periodic industrial slumps; shipbuilding had slowed down and work was scarce. Many Nationalist and British labor leaders, among them the late Prime Minister Ramsay MacDonald, have charged Ulster Unionists with deliberately inciting anti-Catholic violence during times of unemployment to divert resentment from management and Government. "Whenever there is an attempt to root out [sweatshops] in Belfast, the Orange big drum is beaten," MacDonald once said in a House of Commons speech. "Whilst the poor working classes imagine that this is religious trouble, the people who pay the piper know perfectly well that it is an economic trouble. . . ."

Economic distress was similarly a contributing cause of the disturbances in Northern Ireland in 1968 and 1969. Early in October 1968, during an unauthorized Catholic civil rights march in Londonderry, the embittered marchers clashed in bloody fighting with intransigent Protestants. Nearly 100 persons were injured in the two days of rioting. In the following months the Government took some overdue steps towards a fairer allocation of housing and even acquiesced to the demand of "one man one vote." The lateness of the concessions had in the meantime brought to the fore a more radical faction of the Catholic opposition and the slogan "one man one vote" had turned into "one man one job" and "one family one house."

Tension between the opposing extremist groups rose during the summer of 1969, and a parade, celebrating the Protestant victory of 1690, ended in a bloody battle in the Bogside, a Londonderry slum area inhabited by Catholics. The rock and gasoline-bomb throwing rioters were urged on by Bernadette Devlin, a 22-year-old Catholic radical recently elected to the British Parliament. The violence spread to Belfast and a total of nine persons were killed and 500 injured. Unable to restore order, the Government reluctantly called in British troops who calmed the sectarian fighting and stayed on to guard vital installations and the fragile peace.

NOT only has there been civil strife within Northern Ireland, but continued bad feeling between North and South over the partition. Any possible chance of conciliation between North and South was ruined in the 1930s, 1940s, and 1950s by the sabotaging expeditions dispatched into Ulster by the I.R.A., an underground, unofficial revival of the Irish Republican Army. In 1962, however, the unofficial I.R.A. officially announced its disbanding, and the border became noticeably quieter.

In the mid-1960s the prime ministers of the Irish Republic and of Northern Ireland met. As a result of their talks, border restrictions were eased considerably and some sort of federal alliance was even vaguely mentioned on both sides of the border. These friendly contacts at the top had little repercussion among the general population of the two Irelands. The Catholics of Northern Ireland continued to feel resentment against the governing Protestants' discriminatory policies in housing, employment and voting rights and, across the border, their co-religionists sympathized with them. However, relations with the Irish Republic to the south seemed to have entered a quieter phase at the beginning of the 1970s. In Dublin, the realization grew that the civil rights battles in Northern Ireland were not just a cloak for anti-partition activities, and that perhaps not all Catholics would accept without question unification with the Irish Republic. Hopefully, the stage was set for a new approach and one that was more sensitive to the social and economic realities and less concerned with the ancestral sectarian feuds.

Angry Outbreak of Old Animosities in Ulster

As a province of the United Kingdom and a stronghold of Protestantism, Northern Ireland has long been beset by two problems: how to deal with its dissatisfied Roman Catholic minority at home, and how to get along with its Catholic Republican neighbor to the south. Of the two dilemmas, the domestic one has been the thornier, for Ulster's Catholics have long complained of political, religious and economic discrimination. The bad feeling erupted in 1968 and 1969 in a civil rights campaign that turned to violence *(right)*, but did force the Government to grant concessions to the minority. Externally the outlook has been brighter, and lingering resentment over the 1921 partition has ebbed in the face of a new conviction that economic progress to the benefit of all can be won only through a lessening of the old tensions.

MILITANT LEADER in the 1969 rioting, 22-year-old Bernadette Devlin had just been elected to Britain's House of Commons as a spokesman for Ulster's Roman Catholics. Her castigation of the police sent in to quell the uprising—she called them "hooligans"—helped get her convicted by a Londonderry court for "riotous behavior," but she announced she would appeal.

BATTLING POLICE, Catholic rioters attack Government forces in Londonderry during the 1969 disturbances. The outbreak occurred after the Government halted a Catholic civil rights march.

KEEPING ORDER, British troops patrol a predominantly Protestant area of Belfast *(below)* after a violent night during which three persons died. Some 8,000 British troops had been sent in.

INDUSTRIAL BELFAST moves with a vigor that has characterized it since the 19th Century

CLOGGING THE STREETS, traffic and pedestrians hurry along Donegall Place, the main artery of Belfast. With close to half a million citizens, Belfast is Ireland's second largest city.

PRESIDING OVER THE METROPOLIS, a statue of Queen Victoria on the grounds of City Hall *(opposite)* surveys the area which became heavily industrialized during Victoria's reign.

CONSTRUCTING A NEW DOCK, workmen add facilities to the Harland & Wolff shipyards, a huge Belfast concern. Shipbuilding employs a critical segment of Ulster's labor force.

ORANGEMAN'S DAY calls forth a throng of marching Ulstermen in Belfast

UNFURLING HISTORY, various lodges of the Orange Order carry banners painted with portraits of their heroes and martyrs as they make the annual walk from Belfast to nearby Finaghy Field on July 12. The procession commemorates the Battle of the Boyne in 1690, which was to extend the domination of Ireland by Protestant England for two and a half centuries.

ROLLING SLOPES provide pasturage for a flock of horned sheep tended by a herdsman above Cushendun, County Antrim. Sheep raising, particularly in the eastern uplands of Ireland, flourishes because of lush grasslands and a long grazing season.

The Farmer's Hard Struggle

IRELAND has made impressive strides toward the industrialization that the country needs for self-sufficiency, but the average Irishman is still the farmer. He represents more than 30 per cent of the working population and produces more than half of the country's total exports. His farm is a small one—so small by American standards that a visitor from Iowa would wonder how he manages to eke out a living.

Experts say that to prosper, an Irish farmer needs at least 45 acres of good land, but 150,000 of the country's 235,000 farmers have less than 30 acres each. (By contrast, the average size of an Iowa farm is 194 acres.) In the poor counties of the west every fourth farm has less than 15 acres. These statistics tend to show that Paddy Dolan, with 37 acres in the fertile midlands near Roscrea in County Tipperary, is somewhat more blessed than most Irish farmers.

Paddy, a calm and cheerful man of 52, finds that hard to believe when he looks at the thatched roof of the four-room whitewashed cottage on his farm where he has raised a family of seven children. He wants to replace the thatched straw with slate, as two of his neighbors have already done, but after 30 years of farming, he was only recently able to put aside enough money for a turf-burning cooking stove. A new roof will have to wait a while. Until the purchase of the stove, his wife Margaret boiled potatoes and baked bread in the cottage's fireplace. In 1962, his best year, the income from the farm was less than the equivalent of $1,500, and he had to pay $120 in taxes.

Paddy can only remind himself, with a prayer of thanks, that he and Margaret are much better off than they were in 1942 when he bought the farm. He had no tractor then, as he has now, and his sons were too small to help with the work. He did all of it alone with one horse and only occasional help from relatives.

TO look back a little farther, the Dolans are figuratively rolling in wealth now. Their previous farm, a smaller place of 22 acres on which they spent nine years, was badly located and drained. Moreover, those were the grim times of worldwide depression and the economic war that broke out after de Valera took office as Prime Minister and refused to pay the land annuities to the British that had been agreed to by the preceding Free State Government. These were remittances for land earlier distributed to Irish farmers by the British.

The British retaliated by raising tariffs that stopped the sale of Irish farm products in Britain and glutted Irish markets and town fairs with unsold cattle. Paddy remembers, with a shudder, taking six dollars for a yearling calf and feeling glad to get the money. The same calf today would bring him $85.

"In those days, a lot of country people in Ireland were living on rabbits," Paddy said a while ago. "Meat in the butcher's shop was sixpence a pound [12 cents] and nobody could afford to buy it. My first year on that first farm of my own, after we were married in 1933, I earned a grand total of £54, around 250 American dollars."

Paddy Dolan's 30-year penny-counting and backbreaking struggle has been the story of the Irish farmer for the past century. It explains why his sons have been forced to emigrate and why most of them stayed in the cities of America as laborers, factory workers and policemen and educated their sons, in turn, to be lawyers, doctors, teachers and businessmen. After the hardship of farm life in Ireland, they wanted no part of the farm in the New World.

There are many related reasons for that hardship, climatic as well as economic. Despite its mild weather, plentiful rain and rich midland soil, Ireland is far from being an ideal farming country. Its steady wetness makes crop-growing hazardous, and in some cloudy summers the hay harvest fails. The best and most dependable agricultural product is the green Irish grass.

The whole farm economy is consequently based on the raising of livestock, especially of the beef cattle that is shipped, most of it on the hoof, to Great Britain. But profitable cattle raising requires more pasture land than small farmers like Paddy Dolan own, and more working capital, for buying calves and cows, than they are able to accumulate.

Paddy's major problem in his early years as a farmer was that he was always forced to sell his calves as yearlings because he needed money to live on. All of his savings and Margaret's small dowry had gone into the $560 that he paid for their run-down 22 acres and small, shabby cottage. He could never hold onto his three cows' young offspring long enough so that they would be worth a substantial price.

NOT until World War II, when the food scarcity sent farm product prices up, was Paddy able to sell two-year-old cattle for the first time. His earnings rose to around $600 a year. It was then, to his great delight, that he sold his badly drained land for $700 and bought his present place near Roscrea for $3,200, borrowing the balance from a cousin in New York, a loan he has now almost repaid.

The next memorable turning point in Paddy's life came in 1960, when he was finally able to make a down payment on his cherished secondhand tractor with the help of an unexpected windfall. He raised an exceptionally good field of turnips and sold a neighbor the right to graze sheep on the greens. He made $210 on the deal.

"I wonder now how I ever existed without a tractor," he says. "The grand thing about it is that when I come in from work in the evening I don't have to unharness it and feed it and carry water to it. I just turn off the key, and walk into the kitchen and sit down to my cup of tea."

Paddy pays off some installments on the tractor by cutting neighbors' hay and hauling their milk to the creamery. He now has five cows, each producing 500 gallons of milk a year that he sells to the creamery, getting back skim milk for his calves and pigs. He maintains a herd of 15 young beef cattle that he sells as two-year-olds. A good Irish two-year-old goes alive to Britain for a few more months of feeding; most of the first-class live beef imported into Britain was raised in Ireland, where the rich midlands grass develops hefty animals.

The Dolan farm also has a flock of chickens, 25 sheep and a considerable number of pigs, including three sows. Some of the pigs are sent to the market in Roscrea and others supply the family with the Irish farmer's favorite and most frequent midday dinner, boiled lean bacon and cabbage, served with potatoes and homemade wholewheat bread. Contrary to the American impression, corned beef and cabbage is seldom eaten in Ireland; corned beef became popular among low-paid Irish immigrants in Boston, New York and Chicago before the turn of the century because it was sold in America then for five cents a pound.

Paddy's two older children, Seamus and Katherine, are now working in London and

WHY PEAT CAN BE USED AS A FUEL

How is peat, which the Irish call turf and which looks like dirt, able to burn readily? Today's peat, which is found in bogs, or wet spongy ground, began its development thousands of years ago when aquatic plants decomposed, their remains forming in layers at the bottoms of ponds. These plants, like all organic matter, contained carbon compounds. The pressure of layer upon layer caused the plant matter to compress into deposits with a high proportion of carbon. As with all fuels, the carbon is the most important element in the burning process. Coal, which has a higher proportion of carbon than peat, burns more efficiently. Indeed, if peat were subjected to greater pressures for a longer time, it would turn into coal. Because there is little coal and oil in Ireland, the nation uses peat as a fuel both in the home and in industry.

mailing home a few pounds a month. They return for visits at Christmas and Easter and during their summer holidays; emigration of Irish children no longer necessarily means the permanent separation from the family that it used to. Most emigrating youngsters go to Britain, not only because it is within visiting distance of their homeland, but because transients from the Republic of Ireland have the same rights in England as British subjects. They need no passports, immigration documents or work permits. Many poorer farmers in Mayo and Donegal ("where they eat the potatoes, skins and all") leave their families for four or five months every year and go to England or Scotland to work as laborers to earn "a bit of cash." Paddy thanks God he has never been forced to work away from home. Being separated from his wife and family for two days, he says, would probably kill him.

Two of the younger Dolan boys, Eddie and Frank, are husky teenagers who share the work on the farm. During the slow winter months, Eddie sometimes gets a month or two of employment as a laborer with the local County Council road gang. The three smaller children, Mary, 13, John, 12, and Ellen, 10, have charge of milking, and of the feeding of baby calves and lambs under the supervision of their mother.

The family has a radio, or wireless as they call it, a necessity on an Irish farm for its weather and livestock price reports, but no automobile; that luxury will come after the slate roof. (Television is a dream of the far-distant future.) The Dolans use their tractor for shopping trips and for hauling peat, their fuel for heat and cooking, from a bog 10 miles away. Paddy pays $2.80 for five and a half square yards of turf that he cuts by hand. The Dolans, however, would not think of driving the tractor to church on Sunday. They ride to Mass on their bicycles, a mile each way, Paddy leading the procession with John on a seat behind him and Margaret bringing up the rear with Ellen's small arms clinging around her waist.

Sunday Mass is an eagerly awaited social excursion for a rural family like the Dolans, who live at the end of a boreen, or side lane, half a mile from the main road. At church, they linger after Mass to exchange news and gossip with neighbors, and Margaret notices which wives or daughters have new hats or coats. Other gatherings that supply dinner table conversation topics are the frequent fairs and cattle marts, or auction sales, held at nearby towns.

The traditional Irish country fair, where cattle, sheep, pigs and poultry are bought and sold, is being steadily supplanted —to the intense chagrin of town merchants and pubkeepers—by the new-fangled cattle mart. A farmer who sells an animal at an auction mart receives a check in the mail a few days later; at a fair, after a more informal and personal transaction, he is paid on the spot in cash, some of which he spends immediately in the town pubs and shops. Storekeepers dread the mart almost as much as that other terrible 20th Century innovation, the supermarket, which they believe threatens them with extinction.

Fair day at an Irish town crowds the streets around the main square with cattle and sheep tended by farmers carrying long sticks trimmed from a tree branch that morning. The farmers put on an elaborate show of indifference that does not fool the buyers for a minute. It is easy for a spectator to distinguish between the buyer

THE BACKGROUND OF THE TINKERS

Although the 6,000 tinkers in Ireland lead a "gypsy life" of wandering freely and camping and grazing their horses on other people's property, they are of native Irish stock and not true gypsies. Strictly speaking, gypsies are members of groups which are believed to have migrated from India to Europe beginning about 1,000 A.D. They speak a language called Romany, which is derived from Sanskrit. At best there are no more than a dozen families of genuine gypsies in Ireland. The tinkers were originally tinsmiths, and their name is probably a rendering of the sound made by a smith's hammer on an anvil. This traditional employment has almost completely died out; tinkers now are scavengers, casual laborers and horse dealers. Most of the tinkers belong to distinct families or tribes, each of which elects its own leader.

and the seller; the buyer—an exporter or a bigger farmer who will feed the animal for another year or so—does most of the talking. The seller turns his back and stares vacantly at the sky until he hears a price that interests him. Bartering for a single cow can sometimes go on from early morning until late in the afternoon, with an insistent buyer working on the outwardly bored but inwardly eager and attentive seller, with the help of two or three persuasive go-betweens.

"You're out of your mind altogether asking £45 for a dilapidated bag of bones like that greyhound you're trying to pass off on us as a cow," the buyer says. "Sure if I paid 35 for her, I'd be paying dearly for every single hair on her tail. Sell her now for 40 and you can have time for a pint and still be home nice and easy before your wife puts the dinner on the table, without the tiresome agony of standing around here in the dust and noise for the rest of the day —and then likely as not walking the damn cow all the way home again because nobody but me would be fool enough to take her off your hands, you can be sure of that."

One of the go-betweens grabs the seller's wrist and tries to slap his hand against the outstretched palm of the buyer, the traditional sign of agreement that a deal has been closed. But the seller pulls his arm away indignantly. "You're all in league with him," he growls at the go-betweens. "Get away from me. I'll not listen to a shilling less than 45."

On the edges of the crowd and the herds of animals are hawkers and pitchmen selling religious goods, household articles and other small items of merchandise, or promoting games of chance. The wandering tinker families that follow fairs all over the country also mingle on the fringes. These Irish gypsies, or traveling people as they call themselves, trade horses and donkeys while their women, wrapped in bright plaid shawls and always carrying small babies in their arms, beg on street corners and at kitchen doors. The Irish Government has made recent efforts to keep tinkers from camping in their covered wagons on country roads by allocating space for them in low-rent public housing developments. But after a week or two of this indoor living, which they regard as unhealthy, the tinkers vanish.

ON Sunday afternoons in summer and early fall, Paddy enjoys his favorite relaxation—he is off with a neighbor who has a car to a hurling or football match. The Irish farmer is a fanatical sports lover. In every country pub, the county's hurling and football teams and coaches are endlessly dissected and criticized, and important games of five or 10 years ago are replayed in detail over rounds of stout and beer. After the provincial elimination games, the national championship matches are held in September at Croke Park in Dublin, cheered by crowds of 80,000 and more. Great numbers of the spectators are farmers in rakish tweed caps, puffing excitedly on brier pipes with metal lids on the bowls for protection from the rain.

The county hurling and football teams are strictly amateur organizations. Hurling, a sort of field hockey played with a thick, curved stick of ash and a small ball, requires a deft skill and fine timing. It is a very fast game, fascinating to watch. Parish teams played it in Ireland more than 200 years ago, with hundreds of men and boys on each side knocking the ball across the countryside. Under modern rules, the game is confined to a field somewhat larger than a football gridiron. The squads have been restricted to 15 men each. The game the Irish call Gaelic football, which has become more popular than hurling, is a combination of rugby and soccer with charging and long kicking, but no tackling.

Because they are such Irish games, hurling and Gaelic football were suppressed in past centuries by the British authorities. They regarded the popular enthusiasm for the sports as a dangerous display of nationalism. The Gaelic Athletic Association, organized in 1884 to revive the games, established a retaliatory rule, still in effect today, forbidding any member of its football and hurling teams to play such British sports as cricket, soccer or rugby. Another defiantly patriotic rule of the Association, now relaxed, forbade its members from even watching non-Irish sports.

When he was younger Paddy was devoted, like a lot of other farmers, to road bowling, a peculiarly Irish game that has been hampered in recent years by the increase in automobile traffic. The bowlers, backed by lively betting, roll small iron balls along country roads, striving for distance rather than marksmanship. They try to cover a certain number of miles in the fewest number of throws.

The Irish countrymen, especially the younger, unmarried men, are avid followers of greyhound racing. Almost every large town has a greyhound track. In the counties of Dublin, Meath, Cork and Tipperary, and at the National Open Cup meeting in Kildare, dogs are raced, as they were centuries ago, across open fields. All of the Irish, country folk and town people alike, flock to horse races run on great sweeping courses of turf like those seen in old sporting prints.

ON the day of the Irish Sweepstakes Derby, the bar under the grandstand at the Curragh in Kildare, which claims to be the longest in the world—it stretches more than 100 yards—is thronged four deep with men reaching over other men's shoulders for drinks and talking about the last or the next race. On every other corner in every city and large town, there is an office of a "turf accountant," the Irish bookmaker's dignified name for his profession. The gala period of the Dublin year, with hotels overflowing and parties every night, is the week of the Royal Dublin Society's August Horse

Show and world jumping competition, one of the most colorful sports spectacles in the world.

While more frequent today, such days of leisure are rare for the Irish farmer. To prosper, even to survive, he must give his time to his land. Paddy Dolan is what Irish agricultural officials call a broadminded farmer; he attends farm association meetings and keeps in touch with the latest theories on land improvement and livestock breeding. He has been observing with interest the recent success of sugar-beet growing in Ireland. The state-owned Irish Sugar Company buys beet crops from farmers on a contract basis and operates four refineries that export sugar. Paddy would be inclined to try beet growing if he had a few more acres.

Since a fine hay crop cannot be counted on every year, he is also interested in building a silo to store a good harvest for the winter feeding of his stock. The Government would pay part of the costs if he constructed a silo, but Paddy would first have to build it before his grant could be approved, and that, of course, would require capital. He plans to accumulate the money by increasing the milk yield from his stock with the guidance of the Government's experts, but he realizes that it will take time and luck to save the money.

"So I go along, making enough to keep me going from day to day, and hoping to put aside capital for the improvements and the extra acreage that my farm needs," Paddy says. "However, I read in a newspaper that Ireland has a lower suicide rate than other European countries and that Irish farmers have less heart disease than their brothers in Boston." But he adds, "I don't have a brother in Boston so perhaps that doesn't apply to me."

A COUPLE of rungs above Paddy Dolan on the economic ladder are the Irish farmers whose more prosperous status can be readily spotted from the road by the appearance of their houses, substantial two-story buildings of brick or stucco rather than small cottages, and their large barns, which are often roofed with new corrugated metal like the barns that can be seen in the Midwestern United States.

Higher yet, at the top of the scale, are the big and well-kept farms with the handsome Georgian homes built in the 18th Century by wealthy Anglo-Irish Protestant landowners. Their large, high-ceilinged rooms contain original, exquisite furniture and bookshelves, filled with beautifully bound 300-year-old volumes of Molière and Cervantes. Many of these manors are still occupied by descendants of the families that built them. They are the titled gentry who exhibit their hunters at the Dublin Horse Show. "The difference between *them* and us," a small farmer says, "is that when they go out of their house, nobody knows where they're going. If we're not home, we're at Pat Mulligan's or Seamus Casey's, but *they* are likely to be in London or somewhere on the Riviera."

A PROSPEROUS farmer with a choice collection of antiques in his home is an old friend of Paddy Dolan named Joseph Purcell, a well-known cattle and horse auctioneer who operates a 228-acre farm with 500 head of livestock in Birr, County Offaly. Joe Purcell feels that the smaller Irish farmer is being left in the shadows by the Government's emphasis on industrialization. "This country is an agricultural one, but all the Government talks about is industry," Purcell says. "We could greatly improve our general economic picture if we took some steps toward improving Ireland's farm marketing system and supplying fellows like Paddy Dolan with a little more financial help. We can produce beef here cheaper than anybody in Europe. Why not take advantage of that opportunity?"

Government economists in Dublin do not go along with the belief that their industrialization plan overlooks the farmer. On the contrary, they say, more industrial jobs will slow the emigration of farm boys from Ireland, build a larger market for Irish farm produce and enable marginal farmers to sell their land and take factory work, thus creating larger farms—and larger farms are precisely what Paddy Dolan and his neighbors need.

In a field behind their homes in County Mayo, five boys practice the old Irish sport of hurling, a fast game similar to field hockey.

A Passionate Love for All Sports and Pageants

Enthusiasm for sports is Ireland's national tonic. A consuming interest in the fortunes of his county hurling team enlivens the arduous life of the farmer. The ennui of the office worker is forgotten as he cheers his favorite Gaelic football team. A love for the country's fine horses burns in the hearts of all Irishmen, from the gentry who ride to hounds to the small plunger who wagers a few shillings with the "turf accountant." Horse trading is a part of many local fairs, and the premier social event in all Ireland is the Dublin Horse Show. From the brave style of the Horse Show as well as from the mayhem of a football match shine forth the gaiety and spirit of what William Butler Yeats called "the indomitable Irishry."

VIOLENT COLLISION occurs between Galway players (dark jerseys) and Dubliners during the 1963 All-Ireland finals.

HOMETOWN PLAYER is carried from the field *(below)* by Dublin fans after an upset victory over the Galway team.

EXUBERANT SPECTATORS wearing the colors of County Kerry *(opposite)* cheer their team during a match.

GAELIC FOOTBALL, *dating from medieval times, attracts partisan crowds*

YOUNG EQUESTRIENNE, Miss Antoinetta O'Regan, hugs her pony while talking to friends in the stables at the Dublin Horse Show. The Show has several events for fledgling riders.

CROUCHING COMPETITOR takes a handsome horse over a water jump *(below)* as a top-hatted steward looks on. Participants from half a dozen nations compete regularly at the Show.

DUBLIN'S HORSE SHOW, held
*every summer, draws riders and
horse lovers from all over Europe*

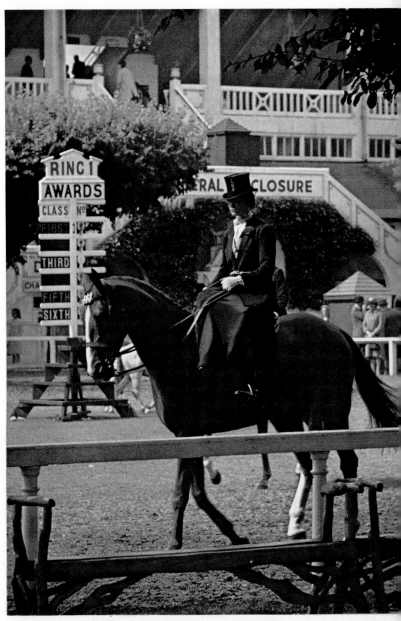

ELEGANT ARISTOCRAT Althea Urquhart, riding sidesaddle in traditional top hat and hunting dress, parades her hunter, Edmund Spenser, during an event on the Show's Ladies' Day.

NATIONAL JUMPING TEAMS heralded by a pipe band *(left)* parade past the flower-bordered stands before competing for the Aga Khan Trophy. The Irish won the trophy in 1963.

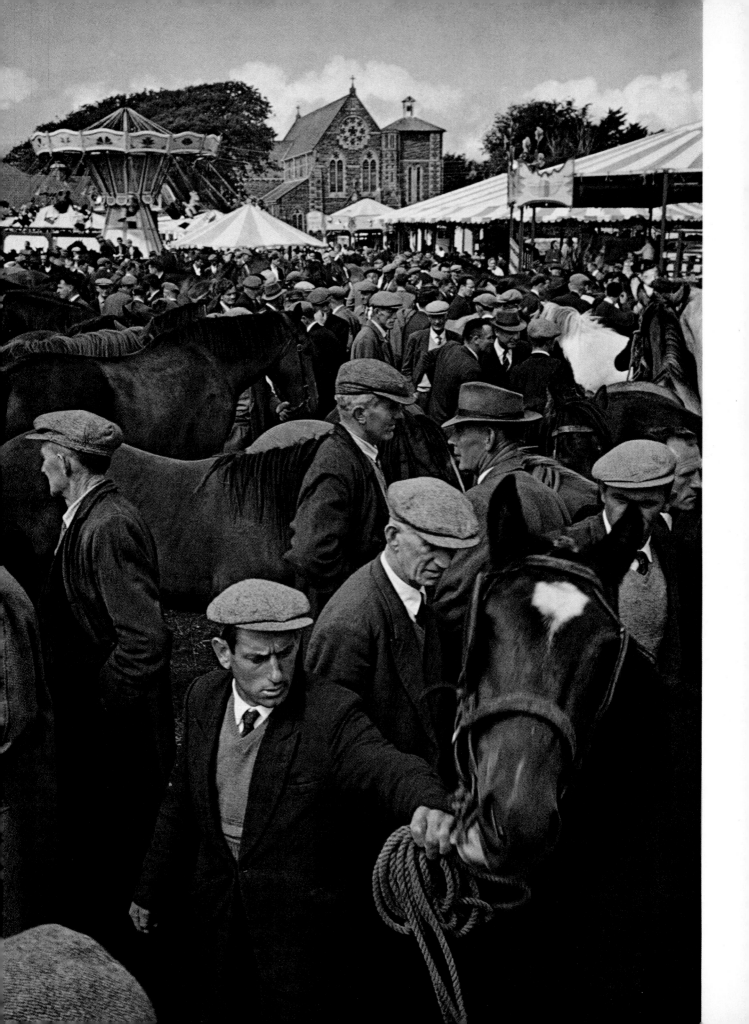

*PUCK FAIR, a mixture
of carnival and hard-headed commerce,
is held each August in Killorglin*

HONORED GOAT which will preside as "King" of Puck Fair is adorned by the Queen, wearing her crown, and her helpers before it is hoisted aloft on a platform in the town square.

EXPERIENCED HORSE TRADERS turn a critical eye on each other's offerings *(opposite)* during the second day of Puck Fair. The Fair offers both carnival rides and wide-open pubs.

HERDS OF CATTLE, unnoticed by men gathered in a pub door, rumble through the streets of Killorglin *(right)* on their way to the livestock market which takes up the Fair's third day.

to hurl an iron ball to a distant finish line

AIRBORNE BOWLER, Donal Lehane, aims his iron ball toward a fan *(background)* who has calculated the route around a corner. Strong bowlers make throws of 200 yards and more.

GRIMLY INTENT CROWD watches Johnny Creedon wind up to throw his 28-ounce cast-iron bowl in a recent match *(left)*. Road bowling is very popular in the environs of Cork.

COUNTRY-LIFE TABLEAU is formed by Montague Kavanaugh, his wife and their children as they ride a donkey cart on the grounds of Dolland, the Kavanaugh home near Dublin.

EAGER HOUNDS, urged on by red-coated riders *(right)*, ford the River Claddy in a scene reminiscent of the 18th Century as the Meath Hunt pursues a fox across the fertile countryside.

PEACEFUL BOAT RIDE on an inlet that borders part of their magnificent 18th Century country estate, Westport House, is enjoyed by the young Earl and Countess of Altamount.

Dublin, which takes up half of the book—is smaller than that of Brooklyn. Automobiles are almost as scarce; there are only 74 family cars for each thousand people in the population. Many workers in Dublin ride to their jobs on bicycles.

Ireland had no television station until 1961, when the Republican Government-owned and -operated Telefís Eireann opened its modern studios in the Donnybrook section of Dublin. (The Ulster Government has its own television station, broadcasting from Belfast.) Irish television is supported by license fees paid by set owners and its programs are not usually sponsored, but spot commercials are shown during program breaks.

Liam Sheehan gave in recently under pressure from his children and bought a television set, paying like most Irish TV owners an extra $65 for a special aerial that picks up the British Broadcasting Corporation programs from Britain in addition to Telefís Eireann shows. As Liam feared, television has filled his living room at all hours of the evening with neighbors of all ages. Irish television goes on the air around five o'clock in the afternoon on weekdays (a few hours earlier with sports events on weekends) and signs off at 11:30 p.m. Like the BBC, it shows many reruns of American entertainment shows and westerns —"The Jack Benny Program," "The Phil Silvers Show," "The Flintstones," "Leave It to Beaver," "Gunsmoke," "Bat Masterson"—interspersed with live native drama, religious programs ("Benediction of the Blessed Sacrament" every Sunday at six), symphony concerts, and variety programs featuring the rock bands, such as the Royals, the Rebels and the Clipper Carltons, that are the rage of Ireland's crowded public dance halls.

ROCK MUSIC also blasts from the Irish radio, making Maureen Sheehan grumble about the suffering that she believes the United States has been inflicting on the rest of the world. She has laid down a rule that Kathy and Eileen, who are now 15 and 14, must not set foot in a dance hall until they are at least 18 years old. Both of the girls are adept dancers, having picked up the steps from their friends. (A favorite Irish twisting tune is called "Twisting in the Gloaming.")

Liam, like many American parents, is praying that television will not distract his youngsters from the habit of reading. After Kathy and Eileen come Mary, 11, John, 9, and Michael, 7, and then Peggy, 18 months. "They're all bookworms, except Peggy, of course, and I want to keep them that way," Liam says. Maureen and Liam, like many of the Irish, are book addicts themselves. Both of them have read their favorite novel, Tolstoy's massive *War and Peace,* from cover to cover four times. They complain because their local Dublin public library allows only three books a week to each adult cardholder.

THE television set is the Sheehans' only outstanding luxury. Their automobile, a small, four-cylinder Fiat that Liam was able to buy secondhand for $840 with a $560 allowance on his previous car, is for him a real necessity. Unlike American husbands who are away at their jobs all day, Liam, like most Irishmen, takes enough time off from his job at noon to eat his big meat-and-potatoes meal of the day at home. This means, of course, that he drives back and forth to his office twice a day.

The old-fashioned custom of eating dinner at noon and a light supper in the evening may account for the slimness of both men and women in Ireland; a foreign visitor realizes after a few days that he has seen few fat people. Then too, food is not the passion in Ireland that it is in countries like France and Italy. Cooking is a necessary chore rather than an artistic ceremony, and the Irishman will usually eat anything put in front of him without bothering overmuch about its flavor or seasoning.

Maureen Sheehan feeds her family with an economy that would impress many American housewives. She spends around $30 a week for meat, groceries and milk. As insufficient as this seems to be to provide for a family of six children and two grownups, it leaves the Sheehans with only about $43 to cover all their other weekly living expenses because Liam's annual income of $4,000 amounts to approximately $77 a week.

THE Sheehans are able to make ends meet (albeit with considerable financial strain) because the Government of the Republic (which has never recognized the Soviet Union) is more socialistic than it admits. (Along with Telefis Eireann and Radio Eireann, the Government owns Irish Airlines, the country's single electric power utility company, and the Irish peat-fuel and sugar-beet industries and railroads. One third of private industrial concerns are heavily subsidized by the Government.) In the areas of education, housing, medical service and social security, an Irish family with six children in the Sheehans' income bracket gets a big paternal helping hand from the state.

The carrying charges on the Sheehans' three-bedroom home, for example, come to only a little more than $200 a year. The land was sold to Liam a few years ago by the Dublin city government on a 99-year mortgage that costs him only $23.80 a year, and the house was built for $1,600, payable over a 35-year period at $182 a year.

The heavy local school taxes that plague small homeowners in America are unknown in Ireland; the national Government pays the entire public education bill. The city tax on Liam's house and property, another of the Sheehans' larger expense items, amounts to $145 a year. All secondary schools in the country, both academic and vocational, are private institutions, usually religious, but the Government pays a grant for each pupil and 75 per cent of the teachers' salaries. Consequently, the tuition fee for Kathy and Eileen Sheehan in a nearby private high school, with Dominican nuns as teachers, comes to only $42 a year each.

Because of deductions for his six children, Liam pays no income taxes. In addition the Government pays the Sheehans a monthly family allowance for children under 16—ten shillings ($1.40) for the first child, 15 shillings and sixpence ($2.17) for the second one and twenty-six and six ($3.71) for each subsequent child. In the case of the Sheehans, with six eligible youngsters, this adds up to $18.41 a month. All Irish families, regardless of how wealthy they may be, are paid such an allowance. Well-to-do parents save it for their childrens' college education, but Maureen uses hers for her family's clothing.

IRELAND does not have Britain's socialized medical service, but a state health insurance plan, with an annual premium of $49, covers the Sheehans' doctor and hospital bills. A social security payment of $196 a year will entitle Liam to retire at half pay when he is 65.

A conservative-minded critic of the welfare state, asking how a small Government like Ireland's can indulge in such social spending without going broke, may find part of the answer in the Republic's defense costs. The annual cost of the green-uniformed Irish Army of 8,000 men is one fifth of what New York City pays for garbage collection each year. The cost of government generally is infinitesimal in Dublin compared to what it is in Washington. Instead of inhabiting an impressive establishment like the White House, the Irish chief executive, Prime Minister John Lynch, lives in a modest but comfortable house in the suburbs. There are few big public buildings. Government offices are scattered around the capital city in old Georgian houses, where they share office space and mailboxes with physicians, lawyers and insurance brokers.

As Thackeray predicted, most members of the rising Irish middle class are independent but quiet people, not given to either servility or rebellion. The Sheehans' main interests are their family and their home. Ireland's suburbia has little civic or community activity beyond the social life of the parish church, with its amateur theatricals, dances and badminton and bowling leagues. There is some Boy Scouting but nothing like the PTA or the Little League.

"My sister lives in Park Forest, Illinois, near Chicago, and she says the husbands and wives there are going to various organization meetings every night in the week," Maureen Sheehan says. "It's not that way in Ireland at all. We're always at home with our kids, perhaps too much so I think at times. Liam and I have never had a holiday alone together in the 16 years of our married life. When we do get away in the summer, it's an outdoor camping trip to Kerry or Donegal and all the children are with us. Our only vice is cigarettes—two packs a day between us, much more than we can afford, but then we have to do something!"

Liam has never been actively involved in politics, somewhat to the disappointment of his father, a rabid Sinn Feiner who served in action with the I.R.A. during the rebellion and the subsequent civil war. Some years ago the elder Sheehan tried to interest his son in the modern underground "new I.R.A.," dedicated to terrorism in British Ulster to break down the partition, but Liam would have none of it.

LIKE most Irishmen of his generation, born after The Troubles and never having heard a shot fired in patriotic anger, Liam regrets the partition because he feels Ireland urgently needs economic union with industrialized Ulster, but he is against blowing up bridges and customs stations at the border. Furthermore, also like most Irishmen his age, he holds no hard grudge against the British. His industrial plant is British-financed and he works under British bosses, getting along fine with them. "Much better fellows than some Irish bosses I've had," he says. Although he listens respectfully to his father's stories about Michael Collins and Terence MacSwiney and the raids of the Black and Tans, that kind of passionate hatred for the British is something he does not fully understand.

Modern Irish politics, reflecting the sober thinking of Liam Sheehan's industrial middle class, is much tamer than it used to be. There is no longer a strongly anti-British faction to enliven the polemics in the Dail, the national parliamentary arena, as there was only a few years ago. Under the leadership of Eamon de Valera, the dominant Fianna Fail Party carried on the old antitreaty and antipartition Republican crusade of the civil war. It was this group —with widespread popular support—that kept Ireland neutral in World War II, despite the fact that the Dublin Government then belonged to the British Commonwealth as a free state, like Canada and Australia. The opposition party, Fine Gael, represented the protreaty, and somewhat more pro-British, Free Staters of the civil war. James M. Dillon, Fine Gael's leader at the time, was the only prominent Irish politician to take a stand against de Valera's neutrality during the war.

BUT now there is little, if any, ideological difference between the two parties, even though they squabble furiously over domestic policies. When de Valera retired from the Fianna Fail leadership in 1959, moving upstairs to the nonpolitical Presidency, he carried with him the last vestiges of the uncompromisingly anti-British spirit of the revolution. His successor, Sean Lemass, was, of course, himself a former I.R.A. fighter who served a year in a Free State jail after the civil war. Without such a record he would never have gotten the party leader's job. But Sean Lemass realized more than Eamon de Valera ever did that Ireland's economy depends on a friendly working relationship with Britain, its best customer as well as its biggest creditor. However much they may disagree on other matters, the two Irish political parties are joined as one in support of the good neighbor policy with the kingdom on the opposite shore of the Irish Sea. The bond that William Pitt failed to tie with his Act of Union at the beginning of the 19th Century seems now to be knotted by the realities of 20th Century economics, which nobody respects more than the hard-working people of Ireland's new middle class.

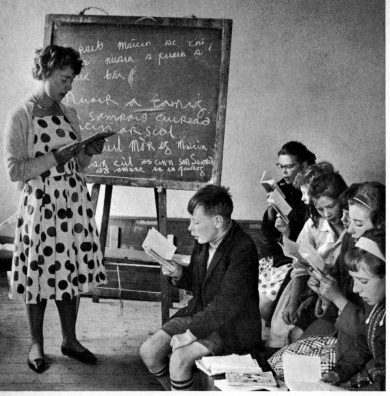

SERIOUS YOUNG STUDENTS in a County Donegal school labor through a Gaelic recitation after putting some Gaelic phrases on the blackboard. Gaelic is taught in all public schools.

Fresh Confidence Breeding New Energy

A new mood of confidence is abroad in Ireland as the country rouses itself from a long period of inertia. Factories are going up, creating new jobs and cutting emigration. Ireland's youth is not only remaining at home, but is also determined to prepare itself, through education, for a role in making the country a modern nation. Heirs to a humanist tradition which was flowering even before the Middle Ages, the Irish have begun to concentrate on such 20th Century preoccupations as electronics and economics. In factories and classrooms a new energy reflects Ireland's turn from self-pity to self-help.

A row of cheerful girls perches on the whitewashed roadside wall before a handsome new school in Newmarket-on-Fergus, County Clare.

AWESOME EXAMINATION HALL of Trinity College, Dublin, rises above a handful of students bending over their exams. Known as the Theatre, the hall was built between 1779 and 1791.

The most renowned of Ireland's colleges, Trinity dates back to 1591 when it was founded by Queen Elizabeth I. It has long rivaled Oxford and Cambridge in excellence of scholarship.

Ireland has a strong educational tradition, and the Government is expending increasing amounts to support and improve the school system.

*A FAMILY in Dublin,
the Boylans live
in modest comfort as the
children energetically
pursue their educations*

A COFFEE BREAK with her friends enlivens registration day *(right)* at University College, Dublin, for Anna Boylan *(center)*, the Boylans' eldest daughter. She is working for a degree in economics.

A NEAT BEDROOM-STUDY surrounds 21-year-old Hugo Boylan *(opposite)*, a serious student of chemical engineering at University College. All four Boylan children attend fine schools or colleges.

AFTER-DINNER DISCUSSION brings together the whole Boylan family *(below)* in their comfortable drawing room. The father, Henry Boylan *(far left)*, is a civil servant and a student of Gaelic literature.

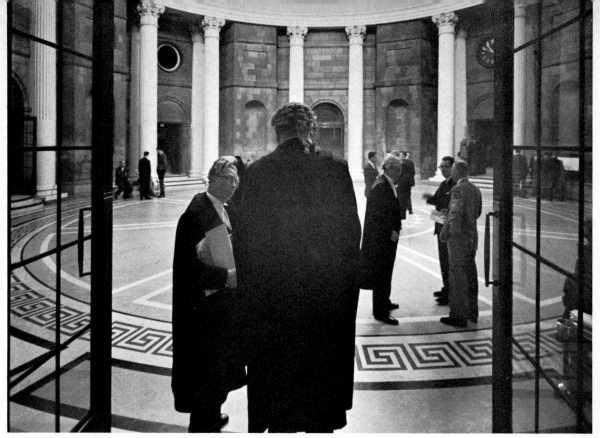

BEWIGGED BARRISTERS greet clients in the columned rotunda at Dublin's Four Courts *(above)*, a magnificent Georgian structure that now houses Ireland's High Court of Justice.

CHEERFULLY BLAZING LIGHTS are reflected in the walls and mirrors of Jammet's restaurant in Dublin *(below)*. Jammet's has been famous for its steaks and the liveliness of its clientele.

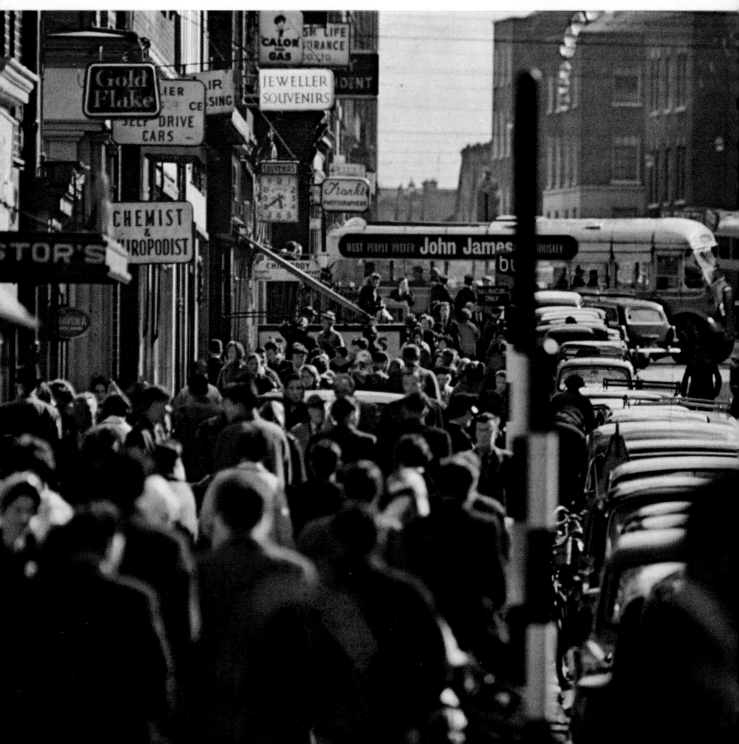

JAMMED THOROUGHFARE, O'Connell Street in Limerick is crowded at rush hour by cars, buses and massed pedestrians. Its 50,000 inhabitants make Limerick Ireland's fourth largest city. With good dock facilities on the River Shannon, Limerick imports many of the materials needed by the plants which surround Shannon Airport and ships much of the plants' produce.

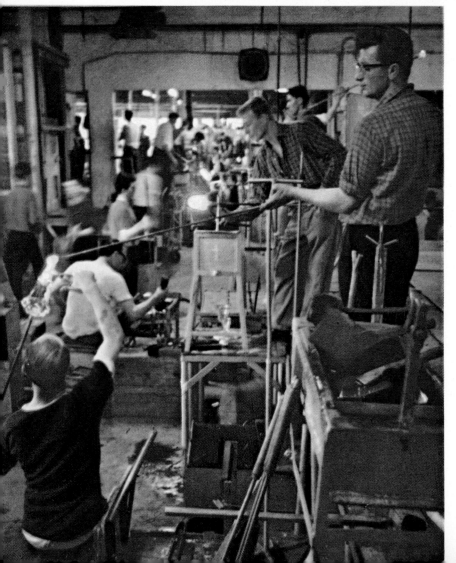

REFURBISHED FACTORY makes the famous Waterford crystal as men shape the molten glass *(left)*. Long idle, the Waterford factory reopened in 1952 with 45 workers. It now employs more than 800.

UP-TO-DATE MACHINE covered with spindles of bright-colored yarn *(right)* knits sweaters for export at a plant near Shannon Airport. Irish knitwear and tweeds find ready markets in Europe and in America.

MODERNITY *comes*
as new plants and
apartment houses rise
and old industries
are revitalized

SLEEK FLATS, housing workers
from the factories near Shannon
Airport *(left),* overlook a customs
shed on the edge of the duty-free
area. Freedom from customs duty
has helped build Shannon's industry.

RIPPLING THE HARBOR, a fishing boat pulls away from a stone pier in Waterford Harbour on a clear spring morning. In the fishing village of Ballyhack, County Wexford, stands a castle *(background)* sacked by Oliver Cromwell in 1649.

10

Ourselves No Longer Alone

THE big change of the 1960s in Ireland, shaping a new course for the future, is the country's abandonment of its stubborn nationalism of the last half century. Seven hundred years of persecution under British rule, climaxed by the bitter memory of the famine, drew the already clannish Irish closer together in hurt resentment long before they won political independence in 1921. When that freedom finally came, it touched off an eruption of suppressed national pride that swelled Ireland with a smug delusion of self-sufficiency.

When the ultranationalist revolutionary leader Eamon de Valera took over the Government in 1932, he launched a 25-year effort to isolate the country as a sort of idealistic refuge of Gaelic culture, aloof from the fast-changing modern world. De Valera waged an economic war against Britain and threw up high tariff barriers against foreign trade in an attempt to promote home industry—while discouraging foreign investments in Ireland. De Valera's protectionist policies had some success. A number of small industries sprang up to supply basic Irish needs, although many of the new firms were inefficient producers and their products were of low quality. Many economists today feel that the protectionist program was basically sound, but carried out with little discrimination. The old leader of Sinn Fein (Ourselves Alone) seemed unwilling to face the hard fact that a small island like Ireland, with no oil and only a little iron and coal in its soil—and no emeralds—could never be industrially self-sustaining.

Trying to stop imports, de Valera even went to the extent of asking the Irish people to drink milk and beer instead of tea, their favorite beverage. The drive against tea was about as futile as his campaign to make the Irish speak Gaelic, still one of the Government's two official languages—English is the other—and compulsory in primary and secondary schools.

THE attempt to revive a native language spoken nowhere in the world except on Ireland's west and southwest coasts and in the highlands of Scotland was, of course, carrying nationalism to impractical extremes. But de Valera persisted in using economic and political pressure to push the change in language. He became so emotionally involved in this crusade that in one public address he declared that the speaking of Gaelic was more important than Ireland's political freedom, an exaggeration that he could not really have meant. The Gaelic language campaign became a symbol of the whole nationalist movement, and the failure of Gaelic to replace English paralleled the realization by the Irish that nationalism could not cure their country's economic ills.

"There seems to be a lot of associations holding meetings and talking a lot about the Irish language," a reader wrote to the editor of *The Connacht Tribune*. "If there was only half as much meetings about jobs for people, the people might be better off. I don't expect any of these Gaelic League people, or whatever they are, care a thrawneen [straw] for my three sons, but I care for them and I would rather hear them speak English as they worked in a Galway factory or in a Galway shop than know they could talk Irish to themselves as they worked on an English railway station."

During the administration of de Valera, covering all but six of the 27 years between 1932 and 1959, emigration steadily drained away Ireland's young people. A general exodus headed for Britain's defense-plant jobs during World War II, while isolated Ireland remained neutral and unstirred by wartime industry. This colony of emigrants stayed on in England after the war, and jobs similar to theirs attracted other Irishmen in the postwar years. "As a result of the demand for wartime workers, there must be more than a million Irish people in England now," an official in Dublin said recently. The emigrants left behind them a country sorely depressed by lack of industrial employment. In a 1949 article about his country, Frank O'Connor wrote, "There is considerable, and sometimes dreadful, poverty. . . . The standard of life is low. The main food of the poorer classes is bread and tea with potatoes and an occasional egg and sausage. . . . Continuous emigration, the feeling that people are fighting a losing battle, induces a feeling of despondency."

THEN, at the beginning of the 1960s, a breath of fresh air swept through the Republic of Ireland. The austere Eamon de Valera, who for all his indifference to harsh economics did more than any Irishman to make his nation free, retired from political leadership in 1959 and was elected to the nonexecutive Presidency. His successor as Fianna Fail Party leader and Prime Minister, Sean Lemass, was a driving industrial promoter. Moving fast to attract foreign investors, the Lemass Government shucked off the hard protective shell of ingrown nationalism. Not only did new industry come in; Ireland came out to join the world.

Signs of a spirited break from narrow provincialism were seen everywhere—in New York and in Africa as well as in Ireland itself. The President of the United Nations General Assembly who called Khrushchev to order when he staged his shoe-thumping tantrum against Dag Hammarskjöld was an Irishman, Frederick H. Boland. In contrast with its past reluctance to become involved in foreign disputes, Ireland shouldered military arms for the U.N. in the Congo. Instead of "The Wearing of the

Green" and the sad ballad of Kevin Barry, the young member of the I.R.A. who was hanged by the British during the Troubles, Irish schoolchildren sang a popular patriotic song about the Irish soldiers who were killed during the fighting in Katanga in 1960.

In fact, observers at the U.N. noted that Ireland was taking up a role of importance in international affairs out of all proportion to its size and political power. Ireland has stepped on the toes of both East and West. It annoyed the French by becoming the first Western European nation to call for self-determination in Algeria. It infuriated the Communists by bringing up the issue of Communist China's aggression in Tibet and irritated others by urging the U.N. to re-examine the question of whether Peking or Taiwan should represent China.

The Irish themselves explain this increasing stature in world politics by pointing out that they have a special position of seniority among smaller countries because their Republic was the first of the modern ex-colonial nations to achieve its independence.

"Such countries as India, Egypt, Algeria and Nigeria trust us and look to us for guidance because we've been through the problems they're going through now," an Irish Government official observes. "Furthermore, they respect us because we've stayed free and clear of deep involvement with the big powers. That's why they feel safe in sending so many of their young people to Ireland for education and political and technical training. If anybody wonders what Ireland's future role in the world will be, there's the answer. As the leader of an increasingly powerful bloc of uncommitted ex-colonial nations, Ireland will be playing a very important role in the years to come."

OTHERS agree, but add that Ireland's prestige in the new nations is not entirely due to their similar political backgrounds. They believe that the Irish missionaries who have worked for many generations in those countries are also responsible for the trust placed in Ireland. Help given in the past by men in Roman collars and women in nuns' habits has not been forgotten.

How long Ireland can remain politically independent of the big powers in the economic pressure of today's world is a matter of lively conjecture in Dublin. A member of an opposition party went so far as to charge in the Irish Parliament that President John F. Kennedy's wildly acclaimed visit to the homeland of his great-grandparents in 1963 was a prelude to the establishment of an American military base at strategically located Shannon Airport.

THE Government shrugs off such speculation, which arises partly from Shannon's economic problems. Before the jet age, it was a thriving refueling stop for transatlantic commercial airliners. The long-range jets can now bypass Ireland on their flights from America to Europe. But Shannon is adjusting by rapidly expanding an already big complex of factories for foreign industrialists within the almost totally tax-free and completely duty-free area of its international airport.

The Shannon offer of manufacturing facilities without taxes or duties is typical of the generous inducements extended by the Government to foreign-financed industries that create new jobs in Ireland. The Republic's Government provides nonrepayable grants covering up to two thirds of the cost of a new plant and its machinery. Some of these subsidies have amounted to as much as $600,000.

Such come-ons are producing the desired effects: Ireland's emigration rate, which reached 56,000 in 1957, steadily decreased during the 1960s and may well continue to fall. The increase in jobs—and the stimulating change in the whole spirit and outlook of the country—is not only cutting emigration. It is also bringing back Irish workers from Britain.

The Government can assure a prospective employer that he can get all the skilled labor he needs merely by dropping a help-wanted-in-Ireland advertisement into a British newspaper. A businessman who manufactures electronic parts in Cork will find plenty of experienced Corkmen in English electronic plants who will jump at the chance to do the same work at home."

John Lynch, who became Prime Minister in 1966, continued to carry out his predecessor's policy of economic development and industrial expansion. One of Ireland's main attractions as an industrial site is the exemption from customs duties that Britain grants almost all goods made in Ireland. Another is the pool of cheap but skilled labor at the disposal of firms that produce for export—primarily British, German and American companies. Irish woolens and tweeds are world famous for their quality, and the export of Irish fashions is increasing, helped along by Dublin's annual fashion show, which attracts buyers from a dozen countries. Ireland's drive to expand overseas trade succeeded, and industrial exports, for instance, jumped from $65 million to $341 million in one decade.

While Ireland's biggest source of foreign exchange during the latter half of the 1960s remained tourism, government planners are confident that the national economic output will continue to grow. One of the underlying reasons for this optimism is the belief that Ireland will become a member of the European Common Market sometime during the early 1970s.

The slightest suggestion of a completely free trading agreement with other Western European countries would have horrified most Irish businessmen a few years ago, and it still worries a great many of them. But Ireland's leaders are convinced that the give and take of competition is just the spur that Ireland needs to increase its productivity.

AS Northern Ireland faces the last half of the 20th Century, it also grapples with an unemployment problem that makes it compete for new industry—but for entirely different reasons. Both shipbuilding, the backbone of Belfast's industrial economy for the past 100 years, and the famed Ulster linen trade are declining. The Northern Irish need jobs in other lines of manufacturing to take up the slack. They envy Eire's ability to offer enticing grants and tax benefits to foreign investors.

"That's the great advantage of having your own government," an official in Belfast says. "We can't barter because we don't have the authority to do so."

A provocative question, discussed with relish in Dublin pubs, is what will happen to Ireland's partition if North and South end up as fellow members of the Common Market. Inevitably, the economies of the two regions will become increasingly interrelated. If that happens, some members of the Government argue, the partition will not last long.

THE idea of continuing economic development and Common Market membership disturbs many people, foreigners as well as Irish, who hate the thought of Ireland's leisurely charm and lovely old castles and cottages giving way to the hustle, noise, six-lane expressways and rectangular dwellings of glass and concrete that seem to accompany the arrival of prosperity in every advancing modern country. An elderly Philadelphian gave voice to such fears a while ago while paying a visit to the 12th Century chapel on the Rock of Cashel.

"I haven't a drop of Irish blood in me, but this is my 14th trip to Ireland," he said. "All the other countries in Western Europe—England, France, Germany and Italy—are getting to look like New Jersey. I hope to God they don't spoil Ireland too, at least not for a few more years. Did you read the speech President Kennedy made in the Irish Parliament when he visited Dublin? He said Ireland was never a rich or powerful country, yet since earliest times its influence on the world has been rich and powerful. I didn't always agree with Kennedy, but that's one time he was right. Now, if you'll excuse me, I must go and get a glass of Guinness at a nice little pub I found this morning."

It will be many more years before Ireland's charm and ancient beauty is seriously endangered by the rush of progress. But after seven centuries of persecution and then four decades of groping as a free but lonely and often despondent nation, Ireland is happy to be finding its place in the world and knowing, at last, where it is going.

Young Dubliners pause at the intersection of Bachelors' Walk and O'Connell Street, close to a bridge which crosses the River Liffey.

A NEW MOOD *characteristic of a generation born after difficult times . . .*

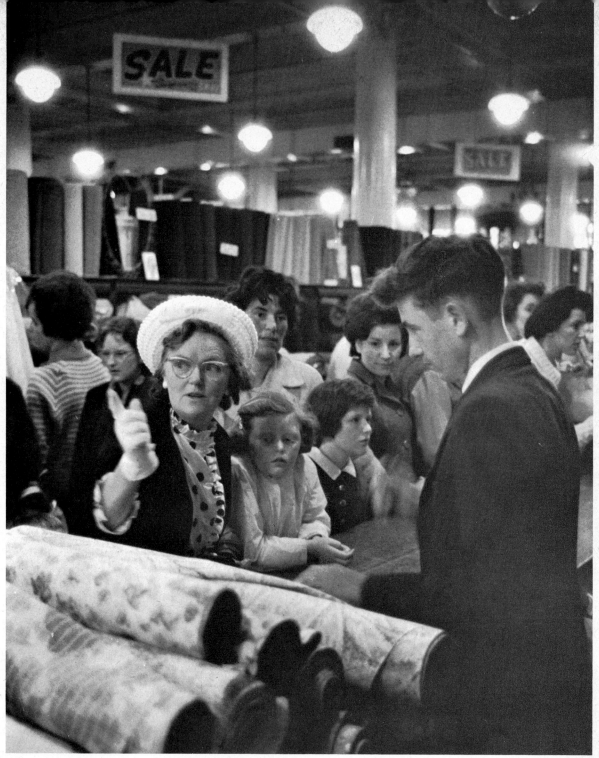

Women of all ages examine fabrics in a booming Dublin department store.

Families pour out of a new Roman Catholic church in County Limerick.

. . . has prepared Ireland to emerge from the apathy and insularity of former days

and enter into the demanding competitive arena of modern industrialized society

Appendix

HISTORICAL DATES

B.C.

c.350 — Gaelic Celts, armed with iron weapons, conquer the island, overpowering a Bronze Age people

A.D.

c.275-300 — Cormac MacArt, of the line of Conn, rules from Tara

380-405 — Reign of Niall of the Nine Hostages, who founds the long-surviving O'Neill line

432 — Patrick, "Apostle of Ireland," begins the conversion of the pagan Celts to Christianity

c.800-1014 — After repeated raids along the coast, Vikings build the first Irish towns

976-1014 — Brian Boru conquers and unifies most of Ireland and becomes High King

1014 — Brian's armies stop a massive Viking attack at the Battle of Clontarf, breaking the Norse hold on Ireland. Brian, however, is slain, and the country falls into disunity

1171 — Ireland is conquered by Normans from Wales under the command of "Strongbow," Earl of Pembroke

1172 — Henry II, King of England, visits Ireland to accept homage from the victorious Normans

1315-1318 — Edward Bruce of Scotland invades the country and is proclaimed "King of Ireland," but after his death in battle, English overlordship is reestablished

1366 — The repressive Statutes of Kilkenny, intended to assure the ascendancy of the Anglo-Normans over the Irish, are promulgated

1495 — Poynings' Law is enacted, which requires that the Irish Parliament obtain prior English approval of proposed legislation

1537-1541 — Henry VIII brings all Ireland under the English Crown and declares himself head of the Church of Ireland

1556 — The English confiscate lands in Leix and Offaly and settle colonists there, establishing the first English "plantations" in Ireland

1569-1603 — Queen Elizabeth I crushes revolts in Munster

1594-1607 — The English put down rebellion in Ulster. The earls of Tyrone and Tyrconnell depart Ireland in fear of English reprisals, an event subsequently known as the "Flight of the Earls"

1609-1610 — In Ulster, the English settle another plantation with Scots and Englishmen

1641-1653 — Rebellion erupts again, simultaneously with the English civil wars. The harsh measures ordered by Oliver Cromwell intensify Irish bitterness

1688-1691 — The Irish support James II, Roman Catholic King of England, in his fight to keep the throne, but he is defeated by an English army at the Battle of the Boyne. Additional Irish lands are confiscated in reprisal for the aid given to James

1695-1727 — The Penal Laws—oppressive measures against Catholics—are enacted

1782-1783 — A patriotic movement by members of the Anglo-Irish ascendancy succeeds in establishing legislative autonomy for the Irish Parliament. Some of the Penal Laws are relaxed

1798 — A rising by the United Irishmen, inspired by Theobald Wolfe Tone and the French Revolution, ends in failure

1800 — British Prime Minister William Pitt pushes through the Act of Union, which dissolves the Irish Parliament, transfers legislative control of the country to London and merges the Irish economy with that of England

1823-1843 — Daniel O'Connell wins a fight for the granting of partial civil rights to Catholics, but his campaign for Home Rule—repeal of the Act of Union—collapses after he capitulates to British directives

1845-1851 — Famine, disease and emigration, brought on by potato crop failures, vastly reduce the Irish population

1848-1867 — A secret, revolutionary group known as the Fenians makes unsuccessful risings in Ireland

1869-1870 — British Prime Minister William Gladstone disestablishes the Protestant Church of Ireland and introduces land reforms

1877-1891 — Backed by Gladstone, Charles Parnell takes up the Home Rule cause but Parnell's involvement in a divorce scandal destroys his popularity

1893 — The Gaelic League is formed by Douglas Hyde to encourage an Irish cultural revival

1904 — Arthur Griffith founds the Sinn Fein (Ourselves Alone) Party

1912-1914 — Home Rule legislation is passed despite opposition in Ulster, but is suspended at the outbreak of World War I

1916 — Forces of the Irish Republican Army seize the Dublin Post Office on Easter Monday and proclaim a republic, but are forced to surrender. Execution of their leaders arouses deep public resentment

1918-1919 — Protests against the conscription of Irishmen into the British Army touch off savage fighting between the I.R.A. and British forces

1920-1921 — Ireland is partitioned. Six Ulster counties receive a separate Parliament. Sinn Fein leaders split over the Anglo-Irish Treaty, which establishes the Irish Free State within the British Commonwealth and accepts the separate status of Northern Ireland

1922-1923 — Civil war breaks out between the pro-treaty faction, which controls the Government, and dissidents led by Eamon de Valera. He eventually calls off armed resistance

1926 — De Valera founds the Fianna Fail (Warriors of Destiny) Party

1932 — Fianna Fail and de Valera come to power. The oath of allegiance to the British Crown is abolished. Economic war with Britain results, each side raises its tariff barriers

1937 — A new Constitution declares Ireland a sovereign state. The British governor-generalship is abolished. Douglas Hyde becomes President

1938 — After compromises on tariffs, the economic war is settled

1939-1945 — Ireland remains neutral during World War II

1949 — The Republic of Ireland is formally proclaimed, removing Ireland from the Commonwealth. Northern Ireland remains a part of the United Kingdom

1959 — Sean Lemass is named Prime Minister and begins a campaign to attract foreign investment. De Valera is elected President

1966 — John Lynch is named Prime Minister

1968-1969 — Disputes over civil rights lead to riots between Catholics and Protestants in Northern Ireland

FOR FURTHER READING

CHAPTER 1: IN ISLAND ISOLATION

Behan, Brendan, *Brendan Behan's Island; An Irish Sketchbook*. Random House, 1962.

Creed, Virginia, *All About Ireland*. Duell, Sloan and Pearce, 1951.

Freeman, Thomas Walter, *Ireland: A General and Regional Geography*. Methuen, London, 1960.

Gorman, Michael, ed., *Ireland by the Irish*. Galley Press, London, 1963.

Killanin, Lord, and Michael V. Duignan, *Shell Guide to Ireland*. W. W. Norton, 1962.

O'Connor, Frank, ed., *A Book of Ireland*. William Collins Sons, London, 1959. *Leinster, Munster and Connaught*. Macmillan, 1950.

Ryan, A. P., *Islands Apart*. William Morrow, 1954.

Waldron, John, *Ireland*. James Duffy, Dublin, 1958.

CHAPTER 2: THE PEOPLE

Arensberg, Conrad M., *The Irish Countryman*. Macmillan, 1937.

Beckett, James Camlin, *A Short History of Ireland*. Longmans, Green, 1952.

Doyle, Lynn, *The Spirit of Ireland*. Charles Scribner's Sons, 1936.

MacManus, Seumas, *The Story of the Irish Race*. Devin-Adair, 1945.

Potter, George W., *To the Golden Door; The Story of the Irish in Ireland and America*. Little, Brown, 1960.

Robertson, Olivia, *It's an Old Irish Custom*. Vanguard Press, 1953.

CHAPTER 3: THE BITTER YEARS

Curtis, Edmund, *A History of Ireland*. University Paperbacks, 1961. *A History of Medieval Ireland*. Methuen, London, 1938.

Curtis, L. P. Jr., *Coercion and Conciliation in Ireland, 1880-1892*. Princeton University Press, 1963.

Ireland, Tom, *Ireland, Past and Present*. G. P. Putnam's Sons, 1942.

Joyce, P. W., *A Social History of Ancient Ireland*. 2 vols. M. H. Gill & Son, 1920.

O'Faolain, Sean, *King of the Beggars; A Life of Daniel O'Connell*. Viking Press, 1938.

O'Siochain, P. A., *Aran Islands of Legend*. Devin-Adair, 1962.

Powell, Thomas G. E., *The Celts*. Frederick A. Praeger, 1958.

Raftery, Joseph, *Prehistoric Ireland*. B. T. Batsford, London, 1951.

Woodham-Smith, Cecil, *The Great Hunger*. Harper & Row, 1962.

CHAPTER 4: THE TROUBLES

Bennett, Richard L., *The Black and Tans*. Houghton Mifflin, 1960.

Brennan, Robert, *Allegiance*. Browne & Nolan, Dublin, 1950.

Bromage, Mary C., *De Valera and the March of a Nation*. Noonday Press, 1956.

Caulfield, Max, *The Easter Rebellion*. Holt, Rinehart & Winston, 1963.

Colum, Padraic, *Ourselves Alone!* Crown Publishers, 1959.

Fox, Richard Michael, *The History of the Irish Citizen Army*. James Duffy, Dublin, 1943.

Gleeson, James, *Bloody Sunday*. Peter Davies, London, 1962.

Gwynn, Denis, *De Valera*. E. P. Dutton, 1933. *The Life and Death of Roger Casement*. Jonathan Cape, 1934.

Horgan, John J., *Parnell to Pearse*. Browne & Nolan, Dublin, 1948.

Macardle, Dorothy, *The Irish Republic*. Victor Gollancz, London, 1937.

Macmanus, M. J., *Eamon de Valera*. Ziff-Davis, 1946.

CHAPTER 5: THE CHURCH

Bieler, Ludwig, *Ireland: Harbinger of the Middle Ages*. Oxford University Press, 1963. *The Life and Legend of St. Patrick*. Clonmore & Reynolds, Dublin, 1949.

De Paor, Maire and Liam, *Early Christian Ireland*. Frederick A. Praeger, 1958.

Moore, Henry K., *Ireland and Her Church*. W. Tempest, Dundalk, Ireland, 1937.

Mould, D.D.C.P., *Ireland of the Saints*. B. T. Batsford, London, 1953.

O'Faolain, Sean, *The Irish; A Character Study*. Devin-Adair, 1949.

CHAPTER 6: LITERATURE AND THE ARTS

Barnet, Sylvan, and others, eds., *The Genius of the Irish Theater*. Mentor Books, 1960.

Boyd, Ernest, *Ireland's Literary Renaissance*. Alfred A. Knopf, 1922.

Carney, James, *Studies in Irish Literature and History*. Dublin Institute for Advanced Studies, 1955.

Colum, Mary Gunning and Padraic, *Our Friend James Joyce*. Doubleday, 1958.

Colum, Padraic, ed., *Treasury of Irish Folklore*. Crown Publishers, 1954.

Corkery, Daniel, *The Hidden Ireland*. M. H. Gill and Son, Dublin, 1956.

Curtayne, Alice, *The Irish Story*. P. J. Kenedy & Sons, 1960.

Dillon, Myles, *Early Irish Literature*. University of Chicago Press, 1948.

Eglinton, John, *Irish Literary Portraits*. Macmillan, 1935.

Howarth, Herbert, *Irish Writers, 1880-1940*. Hill & Wang, 1959. *Irish Writers, Literature Under Parnell's Star*. Hill & Wang, 1958.

Hyde, Douglas, *The Story of Gaelic Literature*. Talbot Press, Dublin, 1938.

Garrity, Devin, ed., *44 Irish Short Stories; An Anthology of Irish Short Fiction from Yeats to Frank O'Connor*. Devin-Adair, 1955. *The Irish Genius*. Mentor Books, 1960.

Gwynn, Stephen, *Irish Literature and Drama in the English Language*. Thomas Nelson & Sons, 1936.

Henry, Françoise, *Irish Art in the Early Period*. Methuen, London, 1940.

Hoagland, Kathleen, ed., *1,000 Years of Irish Poetry*. Devin-Adair, 1947.

Jeffares, A. Norman, *W. B. Yeats: Man and Poet*. Yale University Press, 1949.

Joyce, Stanislaus, *My Brother's Keeper; James Joyce's Early Years*. Viking Press, 1958.

Leask, Harold G., *Irish Castles*. Dundalgan Press, Dundalk, Ireland, 1951. *Irish Churches and Monastic Buildings*. 3 vols., 1955-1960.

MacDonagh, Donagh, and Lennox Robinson, eds., *The Oxford Book of Irish Verse, 17th-20th Century*. Oxford University Press, 1958.

MacManus, Seumas, *Hibernian Nights*. Macmillan, 1963.

Mercier, Vivian, and David H. Greene, eds., *1,000 Years of Irish Prose*. Universal Library, 1961.

O'Connor, Frank, ed., *Modern Irish Short Stories*. Oxford University Press, 1957.

O'Sullivan, Donald, ed., *Songs of the Irish; An Anthology of Irish Folk Music and Poetry with English Verse Translations*. Crown Publishers, 1960.

Robinson, Lennox, *Ireland's Abbey Theatre*. Viking Press, 1946.

Simpson, Alan, *Beckett and Behan and a Theatre in Dublin*. Routledge and Kegan Paul, London, 1962.

Tindall, William York, *A Reader's Guide to James Joyce*. Noonday Press, 1959. *James Joyce*. Grove Press, 1960.

Yeats, W. B., *Collected Poems*. Macmillan, 1953.

CHAPTER 7: NORTHERN IRELAND

Carson, William A., *Ulster and the Irish Republic*. William W. Cleland, Belfast, 1956.

Gallagher, Frank, *The Indivisible Ireland*.

Victor Gollancz, London, 1959.

Gywnn, Denis, *The History of Partition*. Browne & Nolan, Dublin, 1950.

O'Hegarty, Patrick S., *A History of Ireland under the Union*. Methuen, London, 1952.

Pakenham, Frank, *Peace by Ordeal*. Peter Smith, 1935.

Shearman, Hugh, *Ulster*. Robert Hale, London, 1949.

Ulster since 1800. Twelve Talks Broadcast in the Northern Ireland Home Service of the BBC. British Broadcasting Corporation, 1955.

Wilson, Thomas, ed., *Ulster under Home Rule*. Oxford University Press, 1955.

CHAPTERS 8 AND 9: RURAL AND URBAN LIFE

Arensberg, Conrad M., and Solon T. Kimball, *Family and Community in Ireland*. Harvard University Press, 1940.

Behan, Dominic, *Tell Dublin I Miss Her*. G. P. Putnam's Sons, 1962.

Joyce, James, *Dubliners*. Modern Library.

Synge, John Millington, *The Aran Islands and Other Writings*. Vintage Books, 1962.

CHAPTER 10: THE FUTURE

Briscoe, Robert, and Alden Hatch, *For the Life of Me*. Little, Brown, 1958.

McCracken, J. L., *Representative Government in Ireland*. Oxford University Press, 1958.

O'Brien, C. C., ed., *The Shaping of Modern Ireland*. University of Toronto Press, 1960.

FAMOUS IRISH CULTURAL FIGURES AND THEIR PRINCIPAL WORKS

LITERATURE

Keating, Geoffrey	c.1570-1646	History of Ireland in Gaelic: *Forus Feasa ar Eirinn*. Poetry
Broder, David (Daibhidh O'Bruadair)	c.1625-c.1698	Poetry in Gaelic
Swift, Jonathan	1667-1745	Satires: *Gulliver's Travels, A Tale of a Tub, A Modest Proposal*
O'Rahilly, Egan (Aodhagan O'Rathaille)	c.1670-1726	Gaelic poetry decrying the ruin of Ireland
Farquhar, George	1678-1707	Play: *The Beaux' Stratagem*
Berkeley, George	1685-1753	Philosophy: *New Theory of Vision, Dialogues, Treatise concerning the Principles of Human Knowledge*
Burke, Edmund	1729-1797	Political philosophy: *Vindication of Natural Society, Reflections on the Revolution in France*
Goldsmith, Oliver	c.1730-1774	Novel: *The Vicar of Wakefield*. Play: *She Stoops to Conquer*. Poetry: *The Deserted Village*. Essays
O'Sullivan, Owen Roe (Eoghan Ruadh O'Suilleabhain)	c.1746-1784	Gaelic poetry
Merriman, Brian	1747-1805	Gaelic poetry: *Cuirt an Mheanoiche (The Midnight Court)*
Sheridan, Richard Brinsley	1751-1816	Plays: *The School for Scandal, The Rivals, The Critic*
Edgeworth, Maria	1767-1849	Novel: *Castle Rackrent*
Moore, Thomas	1779-1852	Poetry: *Irish Melodies*, including "Believe Me, If All Those Endearing Young Charms," "The Harp That Once through Tara's Halls"
Raftery, Anthony	1784-1835	Gaelic poetry
Mangan, James Clarence	1803-1849	Poetry: "Dark Rosaleen"
LeFanu, Joseph Sheridan	1814-1873	Ghost stories: *In a Glass Darkly*
O'Grady, Standish James	1846-1928	Epic history of Ireland: *Heroic Period, Cuchulain and His Contemporaries*
Lady Gregory, Isabella Augusta	1852-1932	Patron of the Irish literary revival. Wrote plays for the Abbey Theatre

Moore, George	1852-1933	Novels: *Esther Waters, The Lake, A Drama in Muslin*. Memoirs: *Confessions of a Young Man, Hail and Farewell*
Wilde, Oscar	1854-1900	Plays: *The Importance of Being Earnest, Lady Windermere's Fan*. Poetry: *The Ballad of Reading Gaol*. Novel: *The Picture of Dorian Gray*. Criticism: *Intentions*
Shaw, George Bernard	1856-1950	Plays: *Candida, Caesar and Cleopatra, Man and Superman, John Bull's Other Island, Pygmalion, Saint Joan, Heartbreak House*
Martyn, Edward	1859-1923	Play: *The Heather Field*
Hyde, Douglas	1860-1949	Literary history: *A Literary History of Ireland*. Wrote original poetry and translated into English such Gaelic poems as *Love Songs of Connacht*
Yeats, William Butler	1865-1939	Founder of the Irish literary revival and a moving force in the Abbey Theatre. Poetry: "Sailing to Byzantium," "Among School Children," "Easter 1916," "A Prayer for My Daughter," "Under Ben Bulben." Plays: *The Countess Cathleen, Cathleen ni Houlihan, Deirdre*. Autobiography, essays
Æ (George William Russell)	1867-1935	Poetry, essays
Synge, John Millington	1871-1909	Plays: *The Playboy of the Western World, Riders to the Sea, In the Shadow of the Glen, The Tinker's Wedding, The Well of the Saints*
Corkery, Daniel	1878-1965	Literary history and criticism
Gogarty, Oliver St. John	1878-1957	Memoirs: *As I Was Going Down Sackville Street, It Isn't This Time of Year at All*. Poetry
Lord Dunsany, Edward John Moreton Drax Plunkett	1878-1957	Plays, novels, short stories, memoirs, poetry
O'Casey, Sean	1880-1964	Plays: *The Shadow of a Gunman, Juno and the Paycock, The Plough and the Stars*. Autobiography
Colum, Padraic	1881-	Poetry: *Wild Earth*. Plays, stories, novels, essays
Joyce, James	1882-1941	Novels: *Ulysses, Finnegans Wake, A Portrait of the Artist as a Young Man*. Short stories: *Dubliners*. Play: *Exiles*. Poetry: *Chamber Music*
Stephens, James	1882-1950	Fantasy: *The Crock of Gold*. Poetry
Clarke, Austin	1896-	Poetry
O'Flaherty, Liam	1897-	Novels: *The Informer, Skerret, Famine*. Short stories
Bowen, Elizabeth	1899-	Novels: *The Death of the Heart, A World of Love*. Short stories
Carroll, Paul Vincent	1900-	Plays: *Shadow and Substance, The White Steed*
O'Faolain, Sean	1900-	Biographies of famous Irish men and women: Daniel O'Connell, Countess Markievicz, Eamon de Valera. Novels, stories, essays. Autobiography: *Vive Moi!*
O'Connor, Frank (Michael O'Donovan)	1903-1966	Short stories: *Guest of the Nation, Bones of Contention, Crab Apple Jelly, Traveller's Samples, Domestic Relations*. Novels: *The Saint and Mary Kate, Dutch Interior*
Beckett, Samuel	1906-	Plays: *Waiting for Godot, Endgame, Krapp's Last Tape*. Novels: *Murphy Watt, Molloy* trilogy
Murdoch, Iris	1919-	Novels: *A Severed Head, Under the Net, The Unicorn, The Italian Girl*
Moore, Brian	1921-	Novels: *The Lonely Passion of Judith Hearne, The Luck of Ginger Coffey, An Answer From Limbo*
Behan, Brendan	1923-1964	Plays: *The Quare Fellow, The Hostage*. Autobiography: *Borstal Boy*
Leonard, Hugh (John Keys Byrne)	1926-	Play: *Stephen D.*

ART AND ARCHITECTURE

Hone, Nathaniel I	1717-1784	Portrait paintings and engravings
Smyth, Edward	1749-1812	Sculpture: statues for Dublin's Custom House
Johnston, Francis	1761-1829	Architecture: St. George's Church and the General Post Office in Dublin
Kirk, Thomas	1777-1845	Sculpture: statue of Lord Nelson atop the Dublin memorial monument
Hogan, John	1800-1858	Sculpture: statue of the *Dead Christ* in St. Teresa's Church in Dublin
Woodward, Benjamin	1815-1861	Architecture: the Museum Buildings at Trinity College in Dublin
Foley, John Henry	1818-1874	Sculpture: numerous statues, including figures for the Prince Albert memorial in London and one of Stonewall Jackson in Richmond, Virginia. He also designed the seal of the Confederacy
Hone, Nathaniel II	1831-1917	Painting: land- and seascapes
Yeats, John Butler	1839-1922	Portrait paintings. Father of William Butler Yeats
Orpen, William	1870-1931	Painting: portraits and scenes from Irish life
Yeats, Jack Butler	1871-1957	Painting: impressionistic oils with Irish themes, particularly of circuses, prizefights and horses
Healy, Michael	1873-1941	Stained-glass windows
Keating, Sean	1889-	Paintings: portraits and Aran Island landscapes
Hone, Evie	1894-1955	Stained-glass windows, notably the Crucifixion window in Eton's war-damaged 15th Century chapel
Jellett, Mainie	1897-1944	Stained-glass windows and religious paintings
O'Sullivan, Sean	1906-	Portraits of William Butler Yeats and others
Scott, Michael	1906-	Architecture: Dublin's central bus terminal, TV center and other modern structures
Murphy, Seamus	1907-	Sculpture: bust of Countess Markievicz and a memorial to the Fenian leader, Jeremiah O'Donovan Rossa, in Dublin
Collins, Patrick	1911-	Misty landscape paintings
LeBrocquy, Louis	1916-	Abstract landscape paintings and boldly colorful fabric designs
Scott, Patrick	1921-	Abstract paintings

Credits

The sources for the illustrations in this book appear below. Credits for pictures from left to right are separated by commas, from top to bottom by dashes.

Cover—Brian Seed
8, 9—Brian Seed
13—drawings by Adolph E. Brotman
17 through 21—Brian Seed
22, 23—Brian Seed, Farrell Grehan
24—Farrell Grehan
29—map by Rafael D. Palacios
33 through 37—Brian Seed
38, 39—Brian Seed except bottom left and right; Farrell Grehan
40 through 43—Brian Seed
47—map by Enrico Arno
52, 53—Brian Seed
54—Heinz Zinram for TIME
55—Rex Roberts courtesy National Museum of Ireland—Research Laboratory, British Museum, courtesy National Museum of Ireland
56—Brian Seed

57—Radio Times Hulton Picture Library
58, 59—Radio Times Hulton Picture Library except left; Culver Pictures top right; Brown Brothers
60, 61—Radio Times Hulton Picture Library
69—Joe Cashman
70, 71—Joe Cashman except right; Central Press—Radio Times Hulton Picture Library
72—P. A. Reuter
73—Radio Times Hulton Picture Library—Carl Mydans, Brian Seed
74—Brian Seed
80 through 88—Brian Seed
95—Berenice Abbott
96—by Karsh, Ottawa, Culver Pictures—National Gallery of Ireland
97—Gjon Mili—Jerry Bauer

98—Brian Seed—William MacQuitty
99—courtesy Waddington Galleries—Eric Schaal, courtesy New School Art Center
100—Brian Seed
106, 107—London Daily Mirror—Keystone Press Agency, Press Association Photos.
108 through 112—Brian Seed
119, 120—Brian Seed
121—Alan Clifton
122 through 125—Brian Seed
126, 127—Derek Bayes for SPORTS ILLUSTRATED
128, 129—Toni Frissell except bottom left; Brian Seed
130—Brian Seed
136 through 140—Brian Seed
141—John Sadovy for TIME
142, 143—John Sadovy for TIME except bottom left; Brian Seed
144—Farrell Grehan
149, 150, 151—Brian Seed

ACKNOWLEDGMENTS

The editors of this volume are indebted to the following: William Y. Tindall, Professor of English, Columbia University, New York; the Reverend Sean Corkery, Librarian, St. Patrick's College, Maynooth, Ireland; and J. G. Simms, Assistant to the Professor of Modern History, Trinity College, Dublin. Valuable assistance was also provided by Juan M. Greene, Council Member and former President of the Irish National Farmers' Association, Jack Loudan of Belfast, Maureen Snowball Green of London and John Nagle of New York.

Index

This symbol in front of a page number indicates a photograph or painting of the subject mentioned.

✦✦✦✦✦

Production staff for Time Incorporated

John L. Hallenbeck (Vice President and Director of Production)

Robert E. Foy, Caroline Ferri and Robert E. Fraser

Text photocomposed under the direction of

Albert J. Dunn